Jayshankar Prasad's

CHANDRAGUPTA

A Study of Reception and Mediation

Celebrating Indian Drama

Jayshankar Prasad's

CHANDRAGUPTA

A Study of Reception and Mediation

Sanjeev Kumar

abc
asia book club
an international publishing house

Published by
Asia Book Club
Post Box 9615
New Delhi 110 058
Ph. 9818755529

ISBN: 81-7851-22-7

Printed at Chaman Offset Press, New Delhi 110 002

Contents

for

my father

Preface

The present work would not have seen the light of the day without the inspiration, and sustained and close attention of my esteemed teacher Professor Sisir Kumar Das. I owe unbounded gratitude to him for suggesting me to undertake the present study and for acceding to my request for his guidance.

I owe an immeasurable debt of gratitude to Professor Jayanti Chattopadhyay for going through the drafts of this work and for giving me her suggestions; to Professor N.D. Mirajkar, Professor Indira Goswami, Dr. Sebrata Choudhry, Dr. Nandita Basu, Dr. P. Balasubramamian, Dr. C. Raveendran, T.S. Satyanath and Dr. Lalita Mirajkar, who enabled me to gain new insights on the subject; to Professor Rajeev Varma who has been a constant source of inspiration; to Professor N.K. Uberoi, Mr. O.D. Tyagi Dr. S.Q.A. Naqvi and Mr. Naresh Sharma, CPDHE for their affection and encouragement.

The concluding note of this fiesta of thanksgiving deserves a mention of an all-important person—my father. His moral support, love, guidance, philosophic advice and the ever so memorable rebukes which have gone a long way in moulding me as a person with a mission. I dedicate this piece of work to my Papa who single-handedly groomed me to visualize and achieve my goal.

Sanjeev Kumar

Introduction

Since the publication of *Chandragupta* (1931), the twelfth play by Jayshankar Prasad (1889-1937), Hindi critics have found similarities between this play and the Bengali with the same title published twenty years ago, written by the poet-playwright Dwijendralal Roy (1863-1913), which was extremely popular on Bengali stage and was enthusiastically read in the contemporary Hindi literary circles. The question of affinity or influence has been seriously debated by the Hindi scholars for the last five decades or so, and it has not lost its relevance even today if one is interested in the issues of intertextuality and in the contemporary paradigms of influence study. It is necessary, therefore, to start with the examination of the concept of influence in order to place these two texts in a valid theoretical framework.

Theoretical Framework

Simon Juene, who considers 'influence' study central to Comparative Literature writes: "Comparative literature studies, essentially the influence authors, or the literatures of different nations, have exerted on one another, as well as the diffusion of such influences. The national point of departure is never allowed out of sight and these studies often go into minute particulars."[1]

Influence as a literary phenomenon in the Indian situation is unique due to its fact of multilingualism; different languages interacting with each other and in the process creating not only new literary styles but also giving birth to a new language and literature. "There is hardly any other society we know of," observes Das, "where languages belonging to so many families have operated side by side and interacted with each other for so many centuries."[2] And still more significant is the frequent interaction between India and other civilizations. Given the uniqueness of our multilingualism, the inter-intra literary situations, "'Influence' in our case is not confined to two authors or two texts," continues Das, "but is of entire literatures upon each other, and involved with larger questions of socio-political implications."[3]

Trends and tendencies in Indian literature owe their origin to the colonial experience: the colonial pedagogy in the nineteenth century, for example, points out Majumdar "on the inter-literary plane it exerted a direct influence, intra literary transactions in its wake brought about almost simultaneously on indirect influence, which again contributed to no mean extent to cementation of bonds between modern Indian literatures."[4] The concept of 'influence,' however, needs to be distinguished from 'intertextuality.' For one thing, in literary texts, influence can often enter in despite the author. Also, the deeper and more assimilated it is, the more difficult it is, for the author to regulate or for the reader to isolate:

> When influence is assimilated creatively . . . it becomes part of the thought processes, and creative processes, becomes entwined with the works and the ideas of the borrower, and reappears in changed forms. The very changes, in fact, may make it difficult to pinpoint their sources.[5]

The difference between the two concepts is admirably summarized by Jaidev in these words: "One direction awareness in the ephibe can take is intertextuality. In contrast to influence, which largely discounts the individual to influence, volition and will, intertextuality suggests a wholly self-conscious and consciously managed activity."[6] Awareness of influence can lead to intertextuality and its freedom, but intertextuality cannot lead to influence. The law here is similar to the law of gravity. Influence passes into the personality, determines the vision; from the vision to the specifics, the motion is downward. Intertextuality, no matter how extensive, emanates from details and cannot rise up into the vision.[7]

The implication for the artists' intertextuality serves, influence can dominate the author, intertextuality being the device of demonstrating 'how a new text recycles or rearranges the old texts.'[8]

The study of 'influence' has to guard itself against the pitfalls of 'mechanical' way of discovering 'superficial similarities.' Three caveats, pronounced by scholars themselves having made important contributions to this field of investigation, deserve mention. The first is from Irene's Samuel's *Plato and Milton*:

> In order to appraise the influence of one writer on another, we must start of course, from explicit references. But we need not take a narrow view of the transmission of thought from mind to mind. Only a pedant would lift word after word from another's page, or retain in separate compartments of his mind what he has learned from this source and what from that. A thought once assimilated will readily flow into channels far from its original source. Thus, if Milton truly accepts some definite view from Plato, he is not likely to tag it at every use, much less to name the dialogue or epistle in which he found it. In large part the effect of a writer upon any reader cannot be traced back to isolated passages, the spirit of the whole is more likely to remain with him than a series of excerpts.[9]

The second caveat comes from Henry Gifford, who insists that the most rewarding comparisons "are those that writers themselves have accepted or challenged their readers to make—those that spring from 'the shock of recognition,' where one writer has become conscious that any affinity exists between another and himself. Henry James felt this about Tergenev, Pound felt it about Propertius, Pushkin and Byron."[10]

And last but not the least, there is Anna Balakin's timely warning against over-emphasizing the role of influence:

> One is sometimes led to wonder whether any study of influence is truly justified unless it succeeds in elucidating the particular qualities of the borrower, in revealing along with the influence, and almost in spite of it, what is infinitely more important; the turning point at which the writer frees himself of the influence and finds his originality.[11]

In this context, Bankim's perceptive observations on the uniqueness of *Shakuntala* and *Othello* also deserve to be quoted:

> This play of Shakespeare is like a sea. The play of Kalidasa on the other hand is like a beautiful garden. There cannot be any comparison between the sea and the garden. All that is beautiful and pleasant and fragrant and delicate and delightful are to be found in this garden in abundance. And in this sea one finds all that is deep and complex, dynamic and tumultuous. This unparalleled play of Shakespeare, like the sea itself is raging with the waves of emotions, rushing in speed driven by the winds of love and jealousy.[12]

Jayshankar Prasad: A Life Sketch

Jayshankar Prasad is a phenomenon in the field of Hindi drama who, in the opinion of Nagendra, "stands between two summits of world drama—Kalidasa in India and Shakespeare in the West . . . [and] gave a new turn to drama by effecting a synthesis of the emotive content of Indian drama and the psychic conflict of the Western play."[13]

Born in 1889 in a renowned trading family of Varanasi, happiness was a small episode in Prasad's life. His grandfather Shiv Ratan Sahu and his father, a dealer in high quantity perfumed tobacco (snuff), were men of literary taste. It was a daily routine for the local poets to throng at their residence. At the age of eleven he lost his father and, just after three years, i.e., in 1904, his mother. After his father's death, his relatives set an eye on grabbing his ancestral property—the business establishment. A fierce battle, both legal and extra-legal. Antisocial elements were hired by both sides. This continued for 3-4 years.

During those turbulent days, his elder brother, too, passed away. Now he was alone to bear the brunt of life. The result: heavy indebtedness and business in shambles. But that was not all. He was destined to face tragedy after tragedy. His marital life was cut with the passing away of his life-partner shortly after his marriage. He was persuaded to marry again but as ill luck would have it, the second wife, too, did not survive. It was a shattering blow to him. He, however, was again made to agree by his friends and relatives, particularly by his elder brother's spouse, who bestowed on him mother's affection to enter into wedlock for the third time. Subsequently, he was blessed with a son. But then it was his own turn. At the age of just 48, his own life journey came to an end: he died of tuberculosis in November 1937.

Needless to comment that on Prasad's mental make-up, the agonies, trials and tribulations of his own life made a deep impact. And yet, neither was he subdued nor dejected: "*Pita gaye, mata gayee, gurudev gaye, kandhe se kandha bhira karpran dene wala sehchar simharan gaya, to bhi Chandragupta ko rehna parega*" *(Chandragupta,* 4.5. p. 172).

His domestic circumstances forced him to discontinue his studies soon after his father's death when he was in 7th standard. His elder brother, however, arranged for him private coaching separately for English and Sanskrit which enabled him to acquire sound knowledge of Hindu religious texts, scriptures and classics of English literature. He was a bibliophile and read widely. His knowledge of Hindu scriptures and the milieu of his times stimulated him to learn about India's past history. *Chandragupta*, based on his meticulous compilation of historical facts speaks eloquently for his erudition. In his belief system, he was a Shaivite—unmindful of what others said about him—craving for a blissful life.

He displayed embryo of literary genius early in his childhood days: his first piece was published in 1908. Prasad's tragedy was that he could not endear himself to the literary figures of his times—Mahavir Prasad Dwivedi or Shyam Sunder Das. Dwivedi, in fact, refused to publish his article in *Saraswati.* In reaction he started publishing *Indu* (1909). It seems that he took up the challenge quietly and sincerely. The result of his creativity is that he has left a corpus of literature of all the genres—prose, poetry, drama, stories, novels, and so on. *Kamayani* is one of the most sublime and lyrical epics of Hindi literature which has been rendered into English, Sanskrit and with some of its portions in Russian.

Prasad and His Times

When Jayshankar Prasad entered the literary field, the Orientalist discourse which propounded the theory of Aryan Race and the uniqueness of India's culture was the dominant mode of thought. Indian nationalism was conceived as an all-India ideology which attained greatest achievements in art, literature and religion during the so-called political unity pre-eminently under the Mauryas and Gupta kings. Nationalism and religion were working in close nexus with each other. This development of nostalgia for the Hindu past had also created a schism on religious lines: the Hindu Mahasabha and Rashtriya Swayam Sevak Sangh on the one side and Muslim League on the other hand emerged on the scene during the first quarter of the present century.

With the advent of Mahatma Gandhi as leader of the Swaraj movement, there was a dramatic change all over India. He brought the masses into the national struggle. The Rowlatt Act, the massacre at Jallianwala Bagh, the Khilafat Movement, the Simon Commission, the Lahore Congress, the Round Table Conference, the Gandhi-Irwin Pact—all contributed to the national upsurge. The nineteen twenties witnessed youth and women's participation on a bigger scale. Besides, the issues of women's emancipation and removal of untouchablilty were also in focus.

In the field of Hindi drama, pre-Prasad era was dominated by cheap and vulgar Parsee theatre. After Bhartendu, a noticeable slump in the dramatic creativity set in. There were many reasons behind this, the most important being the lack of talented writers in the field. In the name of drama what was being produced were second-rate pieces, largely imitation of Bengali playwright, D.L. Roy. It was at this juncture that Prasad appeared on the literary horizon and retrieved the Hindi drama.

The Plays of Jayshankar Prasad

Jayshankar Prasad began writing plays in his twenties and has, in all, written twelve plays. On the basis of development of the artifact of playwriting, his works can be divided into three groups: (a) the evolutionary phase from 1910 to 1915; (b) the mature phase from 1921 to 1926 and (c) full-fledged maturity phase from 1927 to 1933.

Sajjana (1911), *Kalyani Parinaya* (1912), *Prayaschita* (1914) and *Rajyasri* (1915) are the creation of his evolutionary phase. The first three are one-act plays.

Sajjana follows the cannons laid down in Sanskrit dramaturgy in which he has used both poetry and prose in *Brajbhasa* and dialogues in *Khari Boli*. The play deals with the mythological episode of the *Mahabharata* where Duryodhan perpetrates atrocities on the Pandavas during exile and Yudhistra and the Pandavas display magnanimity.

Kalyani Parinaya, later revised and incorporated in the fourth act of *Chandragupta,* also follows Sanskrit dramaturgy and dialogues and verses mingled with prose. In *Karunalaya,* he has utilized the famous mythological episode about king Harishchandra and has also used for the first time blank verse. The play ends with Bharat-vakya. *Prayaashcita* which was published in *Indu* in 1914 and later incorporated in the second edition of Chitradhar has omitted and Bharat-vakya altogether and the dialogues are in prose only. The play depicts the character of Jaichand from Indian history and is regarded as the first original Hindi play which has a tragic end.

Rajyasri is Prasad's first historical play. The drama focusses upon Rajyasri, the sister of Harsa and is based upon

Banabhatta's *Harshacharita* and the account of the Chinese pilgrim Hsuan Tsang. The original play had three Acts with benediction (Nandi) in the beginning and the end. In the second edition, despite retaining the basic plot, a whole new Act (IV Act) has been added and the benediction (Nandi) has been dropped. From the point of view of the plot, characterization and the dialogues, the second edition is a mature work.

Vishakha (1921), *Ajatsatru* (1922), *Janmejaya ka Nag-yajna* (1923) and *Kamna* (1923-24) are mature works. *Vishakha* deals with an episode from Kalhan's *Raj Tara-ngini*, although the playwright's imagination has made several innovations in the historical theme. The play has three acts and sixteen scenes. It is in this play that the inner conflicts of characters are visible for the first time.

Ajatshatru is a full-length play with three Acts and twenty-eight scenes. The play unmistakably shows the impact of Shakespeare via D.L. Roy. The playwright discards classical cannons and chooses for its bases the elements of action and conflict, both external and internal. The method of contrast in characterization, which he had employed earlier in *Vishakha*, is more fully worked out in this play. The clown (Vidushaka) of Sanskrit plays has found a place here but is rather weak and ineffective. The play is a tragicomedy, based on Jatak stories, the Puranas and history and deals with the famous historical characters of Magadha right from his youth to his coronation and final change of heart.

Janmejaya ka Nagayajna is a mythological play, based mainly on the *Mahabharata* and the *Harivansha Purana.* Most of the characters are derived from these sources. Only four of them—Manavak, Trivikram, Damini and Shila—are the creation of the playwright. The play depicts the struggle between the Nagas and the Aryans. The Aryan King Parikshat is killed by Takshaka, the leader of the Nagas. Parikshat's son, Janamejaya, decides to avenge the death of his father. The theme of the play is ambition and revenge. The Nagas and the Aryans fight a battle, but reconciliation and peace are brought about by Janamejaya's marriage with Manimala, the daughter of Takshak, and harmony is established between the two hostile communities.

Kamna (1923-24) is an allegorical play which bears the influence of Western thinkers like Rousseau, Tolstoy, Shaw and others, in respect of its philosophy. It is a socio-psychological play and is regarded as precursor of *Kamayani.* By the time we reach *Skandgupta* (1928), Prasad has succeeded in evolving his own idiom. The subsequent plays, *Chandragupta* (1931), *Eka Ghunta* (1929) and *Dhruvasvamini* (1933), establish him firmly and finally as an original playwright. *Skandgupta* is regarded as Prasad's most powerful play in which his dexterity in handling the plot "has few parallels." The play is named after the Gupta king Skandgupta who tried effectively to stem the march of the Huns into India. The hero faces the rebellion of his own stepmother, Anantdevi, assisted by Bhatark and Prapanchbuddhi and the invasion of the Huns under the leadership of Khingli. He fights at least three battles besides having to bear the brunt of many domestic conflicts. The play is indeed a plethora of conflicts—domestic, political, social and religious. In this play, "the concept of tragedy introduced into Hindi drama by Bhartendu was given another dimension by Prasad where the hero in his final victory suffers from his personal tragedy."[14]

Chandragupta is an enlarged version of *Kalyani Parinay* in which the hero Chandragupta is fashioned on the pattern of Sanskrit dramaturgy but the development of the plot, the portrayal of the other characters and the finale do not have anything to do with Sanskrit dramaturgy. The play is based on Prasad's meticulous research on Mauryan dynasty. *Eka Ghunta* is Prasad's serious attempt in writing one-act play, albeit, the poet in Prasad dominates the playwright in him to a great extent. *Dhurvaswamini,* his last play, is a departure in which the influence of Ibsen is distinctly visible. Moreover, it is here that for the first time the playwright moves towards a deeper probe between the relations of husband and wife and dwells upon the possibility and propriety of divorce and remarriage. The play draws its plot from history and is supposed to be based on Rakhaldas Bandopadhyaya's *Dhruva.* An outstanding feature of the play is that it can be conveniently presented on the stage.

Prasad had, thus, come a long way from *Sajjan,* moulded in Sanskrit dramaturgy to *Dhruvaswamini,* moulded in Western technique. The Western (Shakespeare's) influence on him is agalore viz., his emphasis in plot construction on action and conflict, his use of the principle of contrast in characterization, use of soliloquies expressing inner conflict, the discarding of '*Nandi,*' '*Sutradhar,*' '*Purvanga,*' and '*Bharat-vakya*' and the division of act into scenes, the presentation of murders, suicides, battle scenes, fainting, fighting, kissing, embracing, burning pyre and such other devices on the stage, the introduction of the devices of dramatic irony, pathetic fallacy, supernatural elements, the working of destiny and the violation of 'three unities.'

The themes of his plays are drawn from the ancient history of India which extends from the reign of Chandragupta Maurya to that of Harsh Vardhan. His nostalgia for the glorious past is in line with the intellectual climate of his era and is motivated by his desire to arouse patriotic feelings.

D.L. Roy

When *Chandragupta* was published critics pointed out similarity and influence of Dwijendralal Roy, a noted Bengali playwright. His play *Chandragupta* made its appearance in 1911, two years before his death. A writer of farces and mythological plays, Roy shifted to historical plays at the turn of the century. He had a penchant for using historical episodes for his plays but except *Chandragupta*, all of these are on the Mughal period. He has written seven plays between 1905 and 1915, namely, *Rana Pratap Singh* (1905); *Durgadas* (1906), *Nurjehan* (1907), *Mewar Patan* (1908), *Shahjahan* (1909), *Chandragupta* (1911) and *Sinhal Vijay* (1915). In fact, Todd's romantic myth-making about Rajput chivalry and valour directed against Muslim invaders was taken on a large scale in Bengali poetry, drama and novels. Roy had been a roaring success commercially on Bengali stage. Dramatists writing on historical themes acknowledged him as their main source of inspiration. He was described as the "greatest dramatist of India." Perhaps no other Bengali author achieved such quick and immense success in Hindi drama, neither before or after.[15] In his heyday, Roy was known as the Shakespeare of Bengal. It was through his works that the traits of Shakespearian drama were transmitted to Hindi drama. His dramas are interspersed with poems and songs.[16]

Plan of the Present Study

The present study is organized into four sections. Section I deals with examining and evaluating the critical opinions on Prasad's *Chandragupta*; its affinity with Roy's text with the same title. The two subsequent sections purport to scrutinize and assess the evidences: both external and internal. The external evidence is the relationship between Bengali and Hindi drama; Prasad's acquaintance with Bengali literature and Roy, and the role of Bengali literature as a mediator of Western influence and Hindi. The internal evidence is based on construction of plot, characterisation and language. The last section dwells on the ideological perspectives emanating from the texts.

NOTES

1. Simon Juene, *Litterature Generale et Litterature Comparee,* Paris, 1968, p. 39. Qtd. S.S. Prawer, 'Influence, Analogy and Tradition,' *Comparative Literary Studies,* p. 51.
2. Sisir Kumar Das, "Why Comparative Indian Literature," Amiya Dev, Sisir Kumar Das, ed., *Comparative Literature: Theory and Practice*, p. 101.
3. *Ibid*., p. 102.
4. Swapan Majumdar, "The Divine Vapour and the Holy Rapes: Problems of Influence Studies in a Colonial Context," Amiya Dev and Sisir Kumar Das, p. 153.
5. L. Mac Pike's conclusion on Dickens's influence on Dostoevsky. Qtd. Jaidev "Intertextuality and Influence: Connections and Boundaries," Amiya Dev and Sisir Kumar Das, pp. I39-40.
6. *Ibid*., p. 134.
7. *Ibid*., p. 137.
8. *Ibid*., p. 139.
9. Irene Samuel, *Plato and Milton.* p. 3. Qtd. S.S. Prawer, pp. 72-73.
10. *Comparative Literature* (London, 1969), p. 73. Qtd. S.S. Prawer, pp. 72-73.
11. "Influence and Literary Future," *Yearbook of Comparative and General Literature* (1962), p. 29. Qtd. S. S. Prawer, p. 73.

12. Qtd. Sisir Kumar Das, *The Artist in Chains: The Life of Bankimchandra Chatterjee*, p. 124.
13. Nagendra, "Dramatic Art," *Jayshankar Prasad: His Mind and Art*, p. 150.
14. Birendra Narayana, *Hindi Drama and Stage*, p. 196.
15. Jayanti Chattopadhyay, "The Rise and Fall of *Chandragupta*—The Hindi Response to Dwijendralal Roy," Amiya Dev and Sisir Kumar Das, p. 219.
16. In the opinion of Manmathnath Gupta, Dwijendralal Roy is the greatest poet of Bengal. For details Manmathnath Gupta, *Bangla Sahitya Darshan,* p. 214.

Critical Opinion on Prasad's *Chandragupta*

Since the publication of Prasad's *Chandragupta* (1931), *a* considerable body of critical writing has accumulated around it, part of which is concerned with relationship between this play and its precursor, a Bengali play with the same title. However, there is divergence in perception of the scholars over the relationship.

First, there is an opinion that considers Prasad totally immune from the influence of D.L Roy. At the other end of the spectrum is another opinion that tends to see nothing original or creative in Prasad's drama (s). Between these two extremes is the third opinion, the mainstream critique, that accepts impact of the Bengali play in one form or the other.

The first opinion is held by Somnath Gupta,[1] the noted Hindi drama critic. In his opinion, "*Prasad ko chorkar anya sabhi (Prasad ke samkaaleen) natak lekhak inke (D.L. Roy) natakon se kisi na kisi ansh mein prabhavit hue hain.*" (Except Prasad, all the playwrights (his contemporaries) have been influenced in varying degrees by D.L. Roy). But this seems to be an extreme view which has not been elaborated by him. Somnath is too enamoured by Prasad.

The second opinion, also an extreme stance, is held by Krishnanand Gupta and Lakshmi Narayan Mishra. Soon after the publication of the play in 1931, Krishnanand Gupta[2] came out with a scathing attack and wrote a 125 page critique of the plays of *Skandgupta* and *Chandragupta.* The rejoinder came from the stalwart Acharya Nand Dulare Vajpayee, who in his piece "*Swatantra Natya Kala ka Abhas*" (1932)[3] (Semblance of independent dramatic craftsmanship) reprimanded Krishnanand Gupta for his writing the critique out of his personal animosity to Prasad, "*(Krishnanand) ki samiksha ka aadhar bahut kuch bhramak hai. . . . D.L. Roy bahut achche lagte honge. . . . (parantu) Prasad ki natya-kala D.L. Roy ki si bhav pradhan aur ek ras nahin hai.*"[4] (The basis of Krishnanand's critique is quite misleading. . . . I can understand that you (Krishnanand Gupta) have a penchant for D.L. Roy . . . (but) Prasad's dramatic craft is not emotive and monotonous like D.L. Roy.)

In the opinion of Lakshmi Narain Misra,[5] "*Prasad ne apne natakon mein Dwijendra ka anukaran kiya hai*" (Prasad has simply imitated Dwijendra in his plays). This, too, was rebutted by Vajpayee. Vajpayee characterized Prasad's play as reflecting an independent dramatic craft despite his being influenced by D.L Roy: "Prasad has assimilated Roy and Shakespeare's techniques in such a way that 'these external elements appear to be natural and product of his own reflection.'"[6] What he further observes is also important, "*D.L. Roy ne unhe nai disha ka sankeit diya. . . . Prasad ki natya kala ka dwitya sopaan un par pare. D.L. Roy ek pashchatya natya padti ke pratinidhi swaroop Skandgupta aur Chandragupta . . . hai.*"[7]

The mainstream critique manifests two strands: the first considers the play to be genuinely related to its Bengali precursor. Such responses give due credit to Prasad for his historical probing but at the same time argue that he has borrowed from the Bengali drama to the extent that the plot, characterization and even the dramatic craft bear the imprint of the Bengali play. The second consists of those who, while conceding Roy's influence and Prasad's literary awareness about his play, underline that the semblance between the two plays is simply misleading and superficial and Prasad's *Chandragupta* is qualitatively a new play. They argue that by the time Prasad wrote *Skandgupta* and *Chandragupta,* he assimilated Roy's influence creatively.

Prominent among those who have seen the stamp of Roy's play are Gulab Rai,[8] Satyendra Taneja,[9] Bishambar Manav,[10] Parmeshwari Lal Gupta[11] and Bhanudev Shukla.[12]

Gulab Rai, a celebrity in Hindi literary world, has made a detailed comparison of the two plays.[13] He has noted both similarities and dissimilarities between the two texts relating to scheme of characters, characterization, plot construction and ideology. In his opinion, "*In dono natakon ke drishtikon Mudrarakshas se bhinn hai. In dono natakon mein Chandragupta . . . Chanakya ke atirikt apna kuch vyaktitva rakhte hai aur apne porush ke saath apna samrajya sthapit karte hai. Dono hi natakon ne unaani senapati Selucus ki duhita se Chandragupta ka vivah karaya hai . . . in dono natakon mein . . . Chanakya aur Arastu ki chot hai*" (The approach of these two plays is different from *Mudrarakshas.* In both the plays, Chandragupta has his own identity apart from Chanakya and establishes his empire due to his valour. Similarly, the marriage of Chandragupta has been solemnized with Greek general Selucus' daughter. . . . The plays underline the clash between Chanakya and Aristotle).

He has elaborated his point by highlighting similarities in the portrayal of events—Chanakya's scheming, depiction of attack by Selucus, disruption of relations between Chanakya and Chandragupta, Chhaya's image in Malvika and Helen's in Cornelia, etc. The dissimilarities are minor except concerning the fact of social origin of Chandragupta. Gulab Rai's analysis, however, shows that Prasad's work is not imitation of Roy's, "*Yadpi Rai mahoday ki pustak pahle ki hai tathapi Prasad ji ki pustak uska anukaran nahin kahin ja sakti.*" And finally he concludes: "Whereas Roy's play reflects more concern for universal love, Prasad's play reverberates with sentiments arousing feelings of national integration and nationalism."[14]

Satyendra Taneja has analyzed the plot, characterization and technique of the play against Roy's and has reached the following conclusion: "A closer scrutiny of the plays by Roy and Prasad bears out marked affinity insofar as plot and characterization are concerned, the difference in approach notwithstanding. Despite portraying Chandragupta as a *Shudra* by Roy and *Kshatriya* by Prasad . . . (yet this) basic difference in approach has brought about not any significant change in characterization . . . the views of the characters, their articulation, views and response to similar situations—all have been depicted with the same brush. Both of the Chanakyas expound the same ideology . . . in the characterization of Chandragupta, both the playwrights seem to follow identical paths. . . . In both the plays, similarities between Roy's Helen and Prasad's Cornelia are too striking. . . . Simharan of *Chandragupta* has been moulded on the pattern of Roy's Chandraketu. . . . There is virtually no difference between Roy's Antigonus and Prasad's Philips, Roy's Katayan has emerged in Prasad's Rakshas. . . . Chhaya's emotions are discernible in Prasad's Kalyani. . . . From the above analysis, it is evident that Prasad was motivated by Roy to write this play. Despite notable variations in events, the plays display the same perspective. Roy has exercised powerful impact in craft too."[15]

Bishambar Manav feels in the same vein. In his opinion a number of identical events and situations in Prasad's play instantly remind us of Roy's play. While not under-rating Prasad, he maintains that Prasad has taken a lot from Roy's play. He says:

> *Koi maane athva na maane par sach baat to yeh hai ki Prasadji nein Vishakhadatta aur D.L. Roy se poora poora laabh uthaya hai. Mudrarakshas se to kam par Roy mahoday ke natak se atyadhik. . . Itne likhne ka tatparya yeh nahin ki Chandragupta Maurya likhte samai Prasadji Roy mahoday ke saamne patti lekar bethe thei, par chhoti chhoti baaton ke liye kisi vyakti ke naam par pratibha, pratibha ki rat lagana hasyaprad hai*[16] (It does not matter whether one likes it or not, but the fact of the matter is that Prasad has benefitted a lot from *Mudrarakshas* but quite substantial from Roy's play . . . it does not mean that while writing *Chandragupta Maurya,* Prasad got dictation from Roy. Nevertheless, it is ridiculous that for petty things genius is attributed to someone to the extent of obsession).

Another noted critic, Parmeshwari Lal Gupta has found a close correspondence between these plays in the matter of plot and characterization. To quote him:

> *Prasadji ke natakon ki maulikta ne aalochakon ko itna abhibhoot kar rakha hai ki is baat ko swikar karna nahin chahate hai ki un par kisi ki chhaap hai par . . . Mudrarakshas aur Shri Dwijedralal Roy ke bangla natak Chandragupta . . . natakon ki chhaap is natak mein prachur maatra mein hai. Is prabhav ka yeh arth nahin hai ki Prasadji ki pratibha ke nijasva ke is natak mein abhav hai. Unki pratibha ki apni visheshta hai, par weh visheshta maulikta ka sthaan nahin Ie sakti.*[17] (Critics are so much enamoured of the originality of Prasad's dramas that they are not at all prepared to acknowledge the external influence on him, however, . . . *Mudrarakshas* and D.L Roy's Bengali play *Chandragupta* (both) have

exercised profound influence over this play. This does not imply that Prasad's own ingenuity has no role in the creation of the drama. Prasad's talent has its own merit, yet that cannot be a substitute for originality.)

Bhanudev Shukla has also observed close affinity between the two plays in matters of plot and characterization: "*Yadi Rai Saheb ne Chandragupta na likha hota to bhi Prasad ka Chandragupta natak kadachit vartmaan roop mein hota. Shayad Chanakya bhi isi prakaar ka bhavuk sehaj maanav hota. Astu ye to anumaan ki baatein hein. Rai mahodaya ne Prasad ko jo prerna di uske abhaav me sambhaavna yeh bhi hai ki Prasad Chandragupta ki rachna bhi na karte.*"[18] He is sceptical about Prasad's launching his venture in case Roy's play had already not been there.

Dasarath Ojha[19] represents the other side of mainstream critique. He concedes Prasad's receptivity from Bengali play but also considers his play entirely distinct from Roy's. In his opinion, Prasad's inculcating Brahmanism in Chanakya shows that he agreed neither with Roy's versions nor with his characterization. The result was *Chandragupta* written from a new perspective. It is the metamorphosis of Chanakya as the epitome of Brahmanism, the singular achievement of Prasad that has given his play a new identity: "*Yạdpi Dwijendralal Rai ka Chandragupta kuch naveen vichaaron ko lekar avtarit hua tha, tathapi Prasad ko us se santosh nahin hua aur unhone usko kuch aur hi aadarsh de diya.*"[20]

Ramratan Bhatnagar[21] is sure that Prasad was fully aware of Roy's play: "*Isme sandeh nahin ki Prasad Rai ke natakon se poorn roop se parichit the . . . par yeh spasht hai ki Chandragupta Maurya ko chhorkar anya koi natak Rai ki rachna se spasht roop se prabhavit nahin hain . . . dono swachhandtavadi kalaakar hain aur sahitya kala ke marmagya hain. Phalte natakon mein bahut si samaantaaye swata aa jaati hain.*"[22] (No doubt, Prasad had prior knowledge of D.L Roy's dramas . . . but it is certain that none of his dramas except *Chandragupta Maurya* show Roy's influence. . . . Both are . . . romanticist artists and endowed with deep perspicuity for literary forms. Therefore, occurrence of similarities are quite natural.)

Dhananjaya has seen in Prasad's dramaturgy a blend of classical and Western craft. In his opinion, western influence came to him via D.L. Roy's dramas.[23] Concurring with Dasarath Ojha, he also opines that Prasad has excelled his predecessor in creating Chanakya as more sublime and humane: "*Dwijendralal Rai aur Vishakhadatta ke Chanakya se kahin adhik maanviye hai Prasad ka Chanakya. Rai aur Vishakhadatta ne use kewal mastishk diya hai, hridya nahin. Prasad ne use hridya diya hai.*"[24]

Bhagwati Prasad Shukla[25] also feels that while in the matter of plot construction and characterization, Prasad's play shows the influence of both *Mudrarakshas* and of D.L. Roy's. His play is the product of his ingenuity and has a distinct identity.

Kusumkaar[26] holds the same view. Sripati Sharma[27] has observed, "in the matter of construction of plot in *Chandragupta,* Prasad is influenced by D.L. Roy's play." Shanti Malik[28] while conceding D.L Roy's influence maintains that Prasad has assimilated Western and classical dramaturgy to such an extent that he has created his own idiom—an accomplishment in which D.L. Roy failed. Shanti Gopal Purohit[29] thinks that in employing soliloquies, Prasad was influenced by D.L. Roy. Jaganath Prasad Sharma[30] has also expressed a similar opinion.

Maheshwar Prasad[31] has noted marked similarities between the two plays with regard to plot and characterization. His conclusion is that Prasad has borrowed outlines of the plot from the Bengali play but the way he has moulded it through his craftsmanship, historical research and imagination, it has turned out to be a distinct play.

Govind Chatak[32] has examined similarities as well as dissimilarities between these two dramas and on that basis he has no difficulty in accepting the view that before writing his play Prasad must have looked up to the Bengali drama and utilized its material for his advantage. But he doesn't support 'imitation' on the part of Prasad. In his opinion, Jayshankar Prasad's play is the product of his own workmanship:

> *phir bhi Prasad ka Chandragupta nitant maulik natak hai jo Vishakhadatta aur Rai ke krititva ke beech apna prithak astitva rakhta hai . . . romani pravratti, kavyatmak anubhuti aur virat chintan par aadharit Prasad ki jeevan-drishti is natak ko mahakavya ki unchaaion tak utha le jaati hai.*[33] (Yet, Prasad's *Chandragupta* is an original play that has its separate identity between the creations of Vishakhadatta and Roy. . . . Based on romantic attitude, poetic perception and deep reflection and his world-view—all have taken the drama to the epic heights.)

In Birendra Narayan's opinion[34] Prasad was influenced by Roy, but only to a certain extent and whatever the similarities between the two texts these are "deceptive." He argues that Chandragupta's portrayal in a different cast and the difference in the involvement of the two playwrights in shaping their other characters has turned Prasad's *Chandragupta* into a superb piece.

Sudhakar Bhattacharya,[35] a Bengali scholar, has extolled Prasad for his writing an original drama:

> *Kintu Prasad ji Dwijendralal dwara prabhavit hote huye kahi par andhanukritti unme nahin hai. Is vishya mein jo log*

> *Prasadji ko Dwijendralal ka anukaarak maankar unke mehatva ko nasht karna chahate hai, unke saath main ekdam sehmat nahi hoon. Dwijendralal jis prakar paschatya sahitya se anupranit hote huye bhi anukaarak nahin the, Prasad bhi waise hi hai*" (Although Prasad is influenced by Roy, nowhere does Prasad demonstrate a blind imitation. Roy's influence on him notwithstanding, I cannot concur with those who are out to under-rate Prasad, simply because of Roy's ostensible influence. Prasad is, in fact, akin to D.L. Roy who despite being influenced by Western literature could maintain his own identity.)

Another Bengali scholar Jayanti Chattopadhyaya, has given her assessment in these words:

> But it is in his last two plays, *Chandragupta* (1931) and *Dhruvaswamini* (1933) that Jayshankar Prasad finally succeeds in discovering his own idiom. It may seem illogical that one who has been so religiously avoiding D.L. Roy's themes should take up the same story, use the same title and almost scheme of characters at the end of his career. . . . He did not hesitate to use similar metaphors and images. But all these external similarities make the internal difference more pronounced. The characters of the chief protagonists, Chandragupta and Chanakya and their relationship have not been portrayed with the same brush. The messages they propagate are also different.[36]

Rama Sen Gupta[37] has also examined the two plays vis-à-vis each other. She has noted a number of similarities between the two plays. However, she does not think it a derivative of the Bengali drama. To quote her:

> *Rashtravadi drishtikon se hi dono natakon ki rachna huyee hai. Kintu dono ne use vibhin roop mein vyakt kiya hai. . . . Prasad ke Chandragupta mein vivek, dridta evam karmnistha hai tatha Dwijendralal ke Chandragupta mein wahi matra-puja ki bhavaatmak prerna hai jis shakti ke dwara vyakti*

> *asadhya saadhan kar sakta hai. . . . Agar Prasad ke natak mein Chandragupta ki rajyochit vyaktitva tatha Chanakya ka adarsh brahamanatva parisfut ho utha hai to Dwijendralal ke natak mein Chandragupta janani Shudrani Mura ke apmanit hridya ki dhara hi prerak shakti hai jisne Arya-vratta samrajya ki sthapna. . . . Dono natakon mein charitra-chitran atyant bhin roop mein hua hai. Atei natak ke prabhava mein bhi bhinta hai. Natya shilp ki drishti se dono natakon mein kathanak ki shithilta abhaav samaan roop se hai.*" (Both the plays have been written from a nationalist perspective, the playwrights have articulated themselves in different ways . . . while Prasad's *Chandragupta* propagates the message of discretion, firmness and dedicated work, Dwijendralal's *Chandragupta* focuses upon veneration and devotion to mother that inspires and strengthens one's morale to accomplish the impossible feats. What emerges from Prasad's *Chandragupta* is Chandragupta's majestic image of a sovereign and Chanakya as a symbol of Brahmanism, in D.L. Roy's play are the torrents of tears of a humiliated mother—the *Shudra* Mura, mother of Chandragupta—that provides inductive power to establish the empire of Aryavratta . . . characterisation has been fashioned differently in both the plays, hence, the difference in their impact, too. From the point of view of dramatic craft, both the plays suffer from looseness in plot).

II

On the question of affinity or influence between Prasad's *Chandragupta* and Bengali play with the same title by D.L. Roy, critical writing in Hindi can be classified into three groups: First is an opinion which considers Prasad totally immune from Roy's influence. This second view finds nothing original in Prasad except imitation of Roy. However, these opinions hardly carry conviction, given their extreme position. The third view—the mainstream critique—finds a nexus between the two dramas. But the critics differ in their assessment. They are unanimous in their opinion that before writing his play, Prasad must have read Roy's *Chandragupta* and Vishakhadatta's *Mudrarakshas*. However, the hold of the Bengali play has been found more pronounced. The mainstream critique has two categories: the first supports an all-pervasive strong influence of the Bengali play in Prasad's. But that does not imply 'imitation' on the part of Prasad. What the critics suggest is both intertextuality and influence. The second opinion holds that by the time Prasad wrote his play, he had succeeded in discovering his own idiom. According to this view, the apparent semblance between the two dramas is simply misleading and superficial and in the ultimate analysis it is Prasad who himself imposes upon his play.

NOTES

1. Somnath Gupta, *Hindi Natak Sahitya ka Itihas*, p. 174.
2. Krishnanand Gupta, *Prasad ji ke do natak.*
3. Rep. Acharya Nand Dulare Vajpayee, *Jayshankar Prasad.*
4. *Ibid.*, p. 109.
5. Lakshmi Narayan Misra, "*Unees varsh baad,*" Preface, *Mukti ka Rahasya*, p. 25.
6. Vajpayee, p. 108
7. *Ibid.*, pp. 160-63.
8. Gulab Rai, *Hindi Natya Vimarsha.*
9. Satyendra Taneja, *Hindi Natak: Punarmulyaankan.*
10. Bishambar Manav, "Chandragupta," Indarnath Madaan. *Prasad Pratibha and his Prasad ke Paanch Natak.*
11. Parmeshwari Lal Gupta. *Prasad ka Natya Sahitya.*
12. Bhanudev Shukla, *Prasad ka Natya Sahitya.*
13. Gulab Rai, "*Chandragupta ka Tulnaatmak Adhyayan,*" pp. 146-54.
14. *Ibid.*, pp. 146-54.

15. Satyendra Taneja, pp. 235, 238, 243-44.
16. Bishambar Manav, pp. 65-67.
17. Parmeshwari Lal Gupta, p. 96.
18. Bhanudev Shukla, pp. 66-67.
19. Dasarath Ojha, *Hindi Natak: Udbhuv aur Vikas*.
20. *Ibid.*, p. 243.
21. Ramratan Bhatnagar, *Prasad ka Jeevan aur Sahitya.*
22. *Ibid.*, p. 125.
23. Dhananjaya, *Prasad ke Aitihasik Natak,* p. 41.
24. *Ibid.*, pp.109-10.
25. Bhagwati Prasad Shukla, *Prasad Yugeen Natak,* p. 111.
26. Kasumkaar, *Hindi Natya Chintan*, p. 111
27. Sripati Sharma, *Hindi Natakon par Paschatya Prabhav*, p. 138.
28. Shanti Malik, *Hindi Natakon ki Shilp Vidhi*, p. 160
29. Shanti Gopal Purohit, *Hindi Natakon ka Vikasatmak Adhyayan*, p. 163.
30. Jaganath Prasad Sharma, *Prasad ke Natkon ka Shastriya Adhyayan*, p. 244.
31. Maheshwar Prasad, *Hindi Bangla Natak*, pp. 178-79.
32. Govind Chatak, *Prasad ke Natak: Swaroop aur Sanrachna*, p. 153.
33. *Ibid.*, p. 153.
34. Birendra Narayan. *Hindi Drama and Stage*, pp. 152-53.
35. Sudhakar Bhattacharya, *Adhunik Hindi Sahitye Banglar Sthan*, p. 57. Qtd. Maheshwar Prasad, p. 209.
36. Jayanti Chattopadhyaya, "The Rise and Fall of Chandragupta: The Hindi Response to Dwijendralal Roy," *Comparative Literature: Theory and Practice*, ed. Amiya Dev and Sisir Kumar Das.
37. Rama Sen Gupta, *Hindi tatha Bangla Natakon ka Tulnatmak Adhyayan,* pp. 109-10, 132-34.

Hindi Drama and Bengali Drama

It is difficult to visualize an independent development of drama in Hindi as a literary genre in isolation from Bengali drama. For one thing, the impetus to depart from Sanskrit dramaturgy and imbibe Western techniques came from Bengali playwrights. For another, the Hindi drama took a clue and direction from the Bengali playwrights for taking recourse to the medium of history for articulating the problems of the present. And yet, there is hardly any evidence in support of interaction in the sense that the relationship has rather been one-sided: the Bengali being the lender and the Hindi, the debtor.

Lineage of Modern Drama

Remarkably, there is just a gap of few years in the lineage of modern drama in both the languages. It was in 1852 that witnessed the first original play in Bengali language. It was *Bhadrarjun*, the plot of which was taken from the *Mahabharata* written by Tarachand Sikdar. It was followed by *Kirti-Vilas* (1852) by Jogendra Chandra Gupta. Here was an attempt for the first time that a bold departure from Sanskrit dramaturgy and adopting Western techniques was made. In 1858 came out Michael Madhusudan's *Sharmishtha* which has been hailed as "the first genuinely modern play in India." It was followed by his two satiricals *Ekai Ki Bale Sabhyata* and *Budo Shaliker Ghare Ron* (1860).

The Hindi drama set about its course with the translation of a Bengali play. The translator was Bhartendu Harishchandra, the father of modern Hindi drama, who wrote *Vidya Sundar*, a loose translation (*Chhayaa anuvaad*) of a Bengali play (written by Maharaja Yatindra Nath Tagore on the basis of *Chaura-Panchasika*).[1]

In the initial phase, the pace of playwriting displayed wide disparity. While up to 1868, just two plays—*Nihusa* and *Shakuntala*—came out in Hindi, the number of Bengali plays over this period soared as high as ninety nine.[2] The reasons for such a hiatus could be traced to the distinctiveness of the socio-cultural and political setting of the two regions, their ethos, heritage, impact or colonial exploitation, level of cultural consciousness, theatrical traditions and so on.

The Hindi region had come under colonial control long after the penetration of Bengal by English administration, language and education had taken place. The development of Allahabad as a seat of literature and journalism started only during the last years of the nineteenth century: the University at Allahabad was the last one to be established in the 19th century (1887) by the British administration. Bengali drama went in close association with reform movements. The mythological dramas in particular and social plays were influenced by the liberal religious preaching of reform movements.

Arya Samaj

The reform movements in Hindi region was spearheaded by Arya Samaj. The task of propagating the Nagri script and Hindi was linked with the Arya Samaj movement. Revivalism was its ideology. But the difference here with the 'reform' movements was of degree rather than kind;[3] Its impact on the development of Hindi drama was a mixed one. A number of playwrights emerged and wrote plays on issues like widow marriage. The refrain of the plays was 'Hindi,' Hindu, Hindustan.[4] But from the point of view of healthy development, Arya Samaj movement proved counter-productive due to its polemic style, the dramatist gave the impression less of a dramatist and more of a preacher, thus, thwarting and paralyzing the budding artists.[5]

Development Phases of Hindi Drama

The development of Hindi drama has a chequered history: while upto the close of the 19th century it witnessed original translated/ adopted plays by Bhartendu and his contemporaries, the period following it, the Dwivedi period, turned out to be sterile. It was in the Prasad era that Hindi drama picked up momentum and acquired prestige. It goes to the credit of Prasad that Hindi dramaturgy succeeded in discovering its own idiom and could free itself from the influence of Bengali by 1935.

The history of the development of Hindi drama between 1850 to 1935 can be divided into three phases:

The formative phase (1850-1900)

The moribund phase (1900-1915) and

The maturity phase (1915-1935)

The Formative Phase

Trends in Bengali Drama

First, we deal with the development in Bengali drama. From 1853, Bengali playwrights followed two distinct patterns: one, the translation and adaptation of English plays, specially those of Shakespeare's and two, the translation and adaptation of the better known Sanskrit plays. The development of Bengali drama was initially influenced by 'reform movements.' It was then taken over by a new patriotic mood. The National Theatre ushered in existence in December 1982 with the staging of *Neeldarpan* (1860), a play by Dina Bandhu Mitra (1829-73) which acquired widespread reputation for its powerful and heart-rending depiction of human suffering. The play was translated into English by Michael Madhusudan Dutt and published by Revd. James Long, a Christian missionary who identified himself with the cause of Bengali peasants. Long was prosecuted and imprisoned. The English version of the play was immediately banned.[7] The National Theatre staged plays designed to expose the atrocities and hollowness of the British administration.[8]

With the establishment of the National Theatre, there was a spurt in playwriting. The Bengali drama witnessed preponderance of lyric drama, mythological, romantic and social plays. But the choice mainly fell on mythological themes: it was the heyday of such plays. This period is known as "Girish Era."[9] The period is marked by the writings of many distinguished playwrights: Girish Chandra Ghosh, Michael Madhusudan Dutt, Jyotindra Nath Thakur, Amrit Lal Basu, Rajkrishan Roy, Ram Narayan Tarakaratna, Dinabandhu Mitra, with many others of a lesser note.

Another field to which the then dramatic literati of Bengali was attracted was the rendering of Western literature into Bengali. Consequently, over this period apart from Sanskrit plays, European dramas and Shakespeare's plays in particular, were translated into Bengali on a large scale.

The Hindi Response

Bhartendu who was fully aware of the developments in Bengali drama made sustained efforts to enrich Hindi by borrowing from the Bengali works.[10] Bhartendu's creative period as a dramatist was 1865-85 but his contribution to drama is unparallelled. He was a visionary and open to new ideas. His interaction with Bengali and Western literature went a long way to shape him so much so that he grasped the futility of adhering to the classical dramaturgy. He observed: "Hence these days, it does not seem logical to write plays based on old theories and values. . . . It is not at all necessary to discard everything that is old . . . in order to present the artifact of writing drama to the best advantage, special attention will have to be paid to the elements of time, place and character."[11] Thus, he hinted at "three unities" of the Western dramaturgy.

Bhartendu's postulate of imbibing freely new ideas led to an outburst of creative activity. A beginning was made in the field of rendering Bengali and Western literature into Hindi. Nevertheless, it was the Bengali drama upon which Hindi leaned. Over this period the response of Hindi towards Bengali found expression in two ways:

(i) Large-scale translations/adaptations of the Bengali plays in Hindi.

(ii) Writing plays on the Bengali pattern

The translations/adaptations of Bengali plays were initiated by Bhartendu himself with *Vidya Sundar*. It was followed by a spate of translations/adaptations.[12]

Sudhakar Chattopadhyaya has listed plays that bear the identical title in Bengali indicating the influence of Bengali—a claim which is not substantiated.[13]

It has been found that despite a large number of renderings, the Hindi authors apparently did not go in for a planned selection—this is evident from the fact that *Neeldarpan* did not find favour with the Hindi translators.

The impact of Bengali drama was not confined to adaptations/translations but it affected dramatic techniques and diction as well. For example, Hindi drama tended to acquire from the Bengali drama such devices as representation of restricted scenes, division into Acts and scenes, Garbhaank use of emotionally surcharged dialogues, concept of personification and curtain etc.

In short, it can be said that the Hindi playwrights might have acquired knowledge of Western concepts of drama through their exposure to English Literature, but was undoubtedly the Bengali literature which enabled them to do so.

The Moribund Phase (1900-1915)

The passing away of Bhartendu (1885) dealt a severe blow to Hindi drama. There was no creative writing for years to come, nor was there any hope of its retrieve. It was gloom all around. Kishori Lal Goswami, a contemporary of Bhartendu expressed his anguish in these words: "Ever since Bhartendu Harishchandra left for his heavenly abode- a spell of disaster has descended on Hindi literature. Perhaps the genre of drama has gone with him."[14]

And the way out? The answer came from Gopal Ram Gahmari, the popular writer of that era—and he was candid enough—that in order to replenish the dwindling stock of Hindi, prop of Bengali literature is a must.[15]

Another writer, Ram Krishna Verma lamented thus: "After Bhartendu's demise the condition of dramas is so pathetic that only those who are familiar with the qualities and characteristics of drama can realize."[16]

The fact of the matter is that conditions in the Hindi literary field were increasingly turning unfavourable to the creation of good dramas. The literary scene was taken over lock, stock and barrel by persons like Devaki Nandan Khatri and Gopal Ram Gahmari who were providing surfeit of just trash from the point of view of literature: sapid, intoxicating and thrilling, but at the same time incapacitating thinking and creative faculty. In the field of drama, it was a barren period, a vacuum and whatever was created was not more than 'old wine in new bottles.'[17]

The vacuum was filled in by the Parsee Theatre—it ruled the roost—staging mythological and social plays and mutilated versions of Shakespeare's drama in a very crude way. This theatre was drawing big crowd and in the absence of a proper leader, the budding playwrights were consciously or unconsciously initiating the technique of commercial plays—a tendency that had been severely criticized by a puritan like Mahavir Prasad Dwivedi.[18]

Heyday of Bengali Drama

In Bengal it was a different scenario. While Hindi drama was languishing at its nadir, the glory of Bengali drama was at its zenith. In those days Bengal was in ferment. The swadeshi mood was sweeping and Bengal was surcharged with feelings of both nationalism and communal harmony. The swadeshi mood in general was "closely associated with attempts to combine politics with religious revivalism."[19] On the other hand, the Brahmo-edited journals like *Sanjivan* or *Prabasi* were critical of obscurantism and bluntly declared that "the patriotism which glorifies our past as ideal and beyond improvement and which rejects the need for further progress is a disease.[20] What is more, Curzon's plan of the Partition of Bengal (1905) had offended the Bengali psyche. The anger and anguish of the Bengalis found literary expression in the songs of Rabindra Nath Tagore, Mukunda Das and Rajnikanta Sen.

In the field of drama, the old stalwarts apart, Dwijendra Lal Roy, Kishirodeprasad Vidyabinode and Rabindra Nath Tagore emerged as the new luminaries. Under the impact of the times, Dwijendra Lal Roy, Girishchandra Ghosh and Kishirodeprasad Vidyabinode along with many minor dramatists switched over to historical plays from mythological, social and romantic operas.[21]

It was against this backdrop that eminent scholar and critic Mahavir Prasad Dwivedi appeared on the scene. He was a man of extraordinary talent and energy and a scholar of Bengali literature. It was his painstaking efforts and sightedness that enabled the Hindi literati to keep into the Bengali scenario to gain first hand knowledge.

As editor of *Saraswati*, he took upon himself the task of publishing renditions of seminal literary pieces of Bengali. The Dwivedi era is known as "Age of Translation." The translation work was not confined to Bengali only. The plays of Marathi, Sanskrit, English, German and French were also rendered. In the Dwivedi era, in the field of drama, Ramchandra Verma and Roop Narayan Pandey translated plays of Girishchandra Ghosh, D.L. Roy, Rabindra Nath Tagore, Manmohan Goswami, Kishirodeprasad Vidyabinode and Jyotindranth Thakur.

This era, which is considered 'sterile' by many, however, carried in its womb, embryo of worthwhile drama. It bequeathed a treasure house of literature of other languages to the rising dramatists who could profitable turn to it for model and inspiration. The emergence of Jayshankar Prasad signalled the end of the moribund phase of Hindi drama.

The tempo of Hindi rendering of the Bengali plays, particularly those of D.L. Roy and Rabindra Nath Tagore, was maintained after the moribund phase.[22] But D.L. Roy turned out to be the most popular, a movement and a phenomenon, Rabindra Nath as a dramatist did not exercise any influence on Hindi drama.[23]

During a short span of nine years (1916-25), all the plays of D.L. Roy were translated in Hindi.[24] A writer of farces and mythological plays, Dwijendra Lal Roy (1863-1913) shifted to historical plays at the turn of the century. Using well-known episodes of gallantry and self-sacrifice from the Hindu and Mughal period, he wrote seven plays between 1905 and 1915.[25] His plays had all the ingredients for popular appeal. They were fashioned after Shakespeare and had emotional appeal and patriotic outbursts. The characters were easier to follow because the plane of conflict was obvious and more earthy. The women of his plays were sketched with kindness and sympathy. Hindu-Muslim unity was a subject which was acceptable to all. And all this in the highly emotional style made its mark.[26] And while Girishchandra Ghosh and Kishirodeprasad Vidyabinode had concentrated mainly on the heroes of Bengal, Dwijendra Lal used incidents and characters that had a pan-Indian appeal. Hence, the choice fell on him.[27] His plays were frequently staged by amateur theatre groups and the students had developed a craze for him.[28]

The cumulative result was that while the prevailing socio-political milieu of nationalism and patriotism motivated the rising playwrights, Bengali drama provided the model. The Hindi drama walked into the footsteps of Bengali drama and trend of utilizing historical episodes, mostly from Hindu past became dominant. There was a harvest of historical plays. As in Bengal, it was the heyday of the historical drama in Hindi too.[29]

Hindi playwrights expressed their gratitude to D.L. Roy acknowledging him as their main source of inspiration. For example, Premchand in the preface to *Karbala*, Chatur Sen Sastri, *Amar Singh* (p. 12), Ugra and Milinda in *Hindi Natakkar aur unke Natak*; *Unki Apne Kalam Se* (*Sahitya Sandesh*, July-August 1955, pp. 93-94); Chandraraj Bhandari in *Sidharath* had expressed their debt to D.L. Roy. Durgadas Gupta and Shivaram Das Gupta have also expressed their indebtedness to him.[30]

Not only that, historical episodes used by Bengali playwrights and D.L. Roy have also been used by Hindi playwrights. For example, D.L. Roy's *Chandragupta* has been used in several Hindi plays: *Chandragupta* (1915) by Badrinath Bhatt, *Chandragupta Maurya* (1931) by Udai Shankar Bhatt, *Chandragupta* (1931) by Prasad and *Bharat Gaurav Arathal Samrat Chandragupta* (1922) by Jineshwar Prasad Mayal.

Again, in a number of cases, the story used by Hindi playwrights has been borrowed from Bengali playwrights. For example, Prasad's *Dhruvaswamini* (1933) and *Skandgupta* have been borrowed from Rakhaldas Bandhopadhyaya's *Dhruva* and *Karuna* respectively. Shaligram's *Puruvikram* is based on Jyotindranath Thakur's *Puruvikram* (1874); *Pratap-Pratijna* (1928) by Jaganath Milinda has similarities with Roy's *Rana Pratap Singh* (1905); Durgadas Gupta's *Desh ka Durdin* is based on Roy's *Mewar ka Patan* (1908); his *Meri Asha* is based on Roy's *Paranpare* (1912); Loknath Shilpkari's *Vir-Jyoti* (1925) is based on Roy's *Shahjahan* (1909). Similarly D.L. Roy's story of a brave chieftain in *Durgadas* (1906) was borrowed by Durgaprasad Gupta for *Mahamaya* (1924), Lala Chhotey Lal Laghu for *Veer Durgadas* (1930), Nathu Lal Bechain for *Atyachari Aurangzeb* (1928) and Swarasingh Varma Anand for *Durgadas*.

The influence of Bengali literature on Hindi was too overwhelming. Sudarshan has described the situation prevailing in 1919 in these words:

> Out of the new publications in Hindi, 95 percent are just rendering. My friend once told me—Hindi publishers are so spell bound by Bengali literature that except Bengali renderings, they don't like any book. If you send them an original text, it is in all probability that they will not agree to publish that. And yet, if it is marked 'Bengali translation,' it is nigh impossible that this will not be gladly accepted.[31]

There is yet another dimension of Hindi Bengali relationship. It is widely acknowledged that Shakespearean technique permeated Hindi drama through D.L. Roy.[32] But in the matter of form and technique, similarities between Hindi and Bengali (D.L. Roy) drama are quite visible. Jayanti Chattopadhyaya has highlighted this point very convincingly. She says: "the metaphor and the epithets are so similar in some passages that the Hindi seems to be a mere translation of the Bengali.[33] She has elaborated:

(a) (i) '*bharat amar bharat amar ke ole ma tum kripar patri*!' (D.L. Roy: India, my India, who says you are to be pitied!)

(ii) '*bharatbarsh hamara pyara bharatbarsh hamara.*' (Badrinath Bhatta, *Chandragupta*: India, Our dear India).

(iii) '*Pyare Rajasthan hamare pyare Rajasthan.*' (Milinda, *Pratap Pratijna*: Dear Rajasthan, my dear Rajasthan).

(b) (i) '*Shirshe shubhra tushar kirit/sagar urmi gheria jangha.*' (D.L. Roy: on her head, the white crown of snow/and around her waist ocean waves).

(ii) '*us par sada him ka mukut subhra sundat suhata.*' (Chandra Kanta Sharma, *Rajsingh*: on it adorns the eternal white crown of snow).

(iii) '*jai bharat jai bharat jai mama pran-pate/bhal bishal charmat krie sit-him-giri-raji.*' (Prem-chand, *Karbala*: glory to India, glory to India, glory to my lord of heart/ your forehead is broad and beautiful with snow peaks).[34]

The picture would remain incomplete without mentioning the undercurrent or the reaction of too much dependence on Bengali drama. The strongest condemnation came from Laxmi Narain Misra who, by his own confession, wrote his first play *Ashok* (1926) under the influence of D.L. Roy.

> *Puraani paripaati se mera matlab Dwijendralal Roy ki natya paripaati se hai—jiska prabhav hamare natakon par bahut bura para. Hamare jo kuch ine-gine naatak idhar prakaashit huye hai, sab durbhagyavash Dwijendralal Roy ko aadarsh maankar lekhakon ne kaagaz rangaa hai. Dwijendralal Roy ne natakon me Bangal ka Shakespeare banana chaha tha, aur Bangali aalochakon ki bhyankar bhaavukta aur dyani-yen vichaarheenta ke kaaran Dwijendralal Roy ko kuch samay ke liye Shakespeare kaa pad mil bhi gayaa. . . . Shakespeare ke anukaran par hamaare desh mein bhaavukta ki gandi pravarti phel gayee aur is gandi pravarti ke sabse bare pratinidhi Dwijendralal Roy huye. Dwijendra Lal Roy se barhkar anthe karan ke andhaa sahityakaar meri drishti me doosra nahin aayaa. . . . Dwijendra ke anoovaad jab se Hindi mein prakaashit huye, swargiya Babu Harishchandra ke natakon ko bachcho kaa khilwar kehkar hamaare sa-hityakaaron ne door phek diya. Dwijendra ke shabdo aur vakyon ka toofan natya kala ka aadarsh ban betha aur jahan dekhiye Hindi ke naye naatakon me Dwijendrawaali banaavti bhasha aur banaavti bhaavukta, sukh, dukh, prem, ghrina, jai aur parajai ke jhoote chitra banne lage hai. . . . Is*

> *Bangali natakkar ki aatmaa ke upar Shakespeare ka bhoot aasan jamaye betha tha.*[35]

However, Hindi was showing signs of overcoming the influence as is evident from Lakshmi Narayan Misra. At the close of the Prasad era, Hindi became free from the overriding influence of Bengali drama.

In the 1930s two personalities of the West took Hindi drama by storm. Henrik Ibsen (1828-1900), the Norwegian dramatist, came to be known through rendering. The other dominating personality was Freud who caught the imagination of Hindi dramatists. The plays of Govinda Vallabha Pant, Lakshmi Narayan Misra, Ugra treaded in the new path. Ugra admitted his break from D.L. Roy in these words: "*Main pahle Bangaal ke mahaan, yashasvi, bahumukhi kalakaar bhi Dwijendralal Rai ko hi sabse bara kalaakaar manta tha, par jab Ibsen ke naatak parhe, tab aankh khul gayee aur spasht huya ki ab tak natak ke naam par jo kuch maine likha hai, weh dusaahas matra hai.*"[36]

NOTES

1. There is an opinion which regards *Nihusa* written by Giridhar Das in 1841 and Rajalaxman Singh's *Shakuntala* (1863) as the first play but by all the canons of dramaturgy Nihusa cannot be regarded as the first play. Bhartendu's play is regarded as the first play in Hindi drama. Maheshwar, *Hindi Bangla Natak*, p. 55 and Satyendra Taneja, *Hindi Natak: Punarmulyaankan*, p. 19.
2. Maheshwar, p. 49.
3. Sumit Sarkar, *Modern India* (1885-1947), p. 75
4. Gopinath Tiwari, *Bhartendu Kaleen Natak Sahitya*, p. 203.
5. Laxmi Sagar Varshney, *Adhunik Hindi Sahitya*, p. 221 and Govind Chatak, *Prasad Natyaa aur Shilp*, p. 7.
6. Sukumar Sen, *History of Bengali Literature*, p. 177.

7. Sisir Kumar Das, *The Artist in Chains: The Life of Bankim Chandra Chatterjee*, p. 15.
8. Amrit Lal Bose and Upendra Nath Das suffered imprisonment for staging *Surendra Binodini*, a drama by the latter. The performance of *Gajanunda*, a farce ridiculing the native stooges of the British ultimately led to Lytton's Dramatic Performance Control Act in 1876.
9. Manmohan Basu, *Bangla Natekar utpatti o kram vikas*, p. 86.
10. Bhartendu termed Bengali "*Sampattishaaleeni gyan vradha barhi behen*" (rich benign erudite elder sister) of Hindi.
11. *Bhartendu Natakavali*, ed. Babu Brajratna Das, Vol. I, p. 431. Qtd. Birendra Narayan, *Hindi Drama and Stage*, p. 16.
12. Bhartendu translated *Bharat-Mata* by Kiran Chand into *Bharat Janni* (1877); Balkrishan Bhatt translated Michael Madhusudan Dutt's *Padmavati* in 1878; Ramkrishnan Verma translated Rajkishore De's *Padmavati* in 1879; Michael Madhusudan Dutt's *Krishan Kumari*; Dwaraka Nath Ganguli's *Vimari*; Udit Narayan Lal translated Manmohan Basu's *Sati* in 1969, Jyotindra Nath's *Ashrumati* (1895) and *Dinirvan*; Pandit Radhacharan Goswami and Ganesh Datta Tiwari made an adaptation of Jyotindra Nath's *Sarojini* and Michael's *Ekai Ki bhole Sabhayata* into *Kya is ko Sabhyata kahte hain* in 1884; Gokul Chand and Radha Goswami translated *Burh Shaaliker Gharhe ro* of Bengali into *Boorhe muh muhaase lok dekhe tamase* in 1887; Gopal Ram Gahamari translated Rajkrishan Roy's *Banvir* and Gopal Chand Mukhopadhyaya's *Yauvan Yugini*; Keshavram Bhatt translated Upendranath Das's *Sharat Sarojini* and came out with *Sajjaad Sambul* (1877) and *Shamshaad Sausan* in 1880 on the basis of *Surendra Vinodini*. He also translated Das's *Dada o aami* into *Dada aur main*; Ramgopal Vidhaat translated Manmohan Basu's *Rambhishek*; Shivandan Tripathi came out with Hindi translation of Laxminarain Chakravorty's *Nawab Sirajudaula* in 1896; Srinivas Das translated *Sayunkta Swyamvar* (1985) and *Prehlaad Charit* (1888);

Radhakrishan Goswami translated Krishnachand Bandhopadhyaya's *Bharat Mein Yavanlog* (1879) etc.

13. Taneja, p. 137.
14. *Jab se Bhartendu ji parlok sidhare hain tab se sahitya ki bari doordasha ho rahi hai. . . . Natak vidha to kadachit Babu sahib apne sang hi le gaye ho.*" See Kishori Lal Goswani, preface to *Chopat Chapeit*.
15. Qtd. Taneja. p. 152.
16. "*Bhartendu . . . ke Swarglok ke baad Natakon ki dasha kuch aisi in dino hain veh kewal ve hi log jaante hain jo Natakon ke Gundosh aur Lakshano se amitya hain.*" Ram Krishan Verma in his Michael Madhusudan Dutt's *Krishan Kumari*, in Taneja, p. 152.
17. Somnath Gupta, p. 90.
18. Jayanti Chattopadhyaya, "The Rise and Fall of *Chandragupta*: The Hindi Response to Dwijendralal Roy," *Comparative Literature*: *Theory and Practice*, ed. Amiya Dev and Sisir Kumar Das, p. 227. Mahavir Prasad Dwivedi, *Natya Sastra* (III ed.), p. 3 and "*Hindi ki Vartman Awastha*," *Saraswati*, p. 470.
19. Sumit Sarkar, p. 114.
20. *Ibid.*, p. 115.
21. For example, Girish Chandra Ghosh wrote *Satnam* (1904), *Vasar* (1860), *Mirkasim*, *Sirajuddaula* and *Chhatrapati Shivaji*.
22. Tagore's renderings were: *Daak Ghar* (1920), *Visarjan* (1924), *Vyang Kautuk* (1924), *Muktdhara* (1925), *Raja Rani* (1925), *Chir Kumar Sabha* (1928) and Munshi Ajmeri's rendering *Chitragandha* (1928).
23. Birendera Narayana, *Hindi Drama and Stage*, p. 81.
24. Somnath Gupta, *Hindi natak Sahitya ka Itihas*, p. 173.
25. *Rana Pratap Singh* (1905), *Durgadas* (1906), *Nurjahan* (1907), *Mewar Patan* (1908), *Shahjahan* (1909), *Chandragupta* (1911) and *Sinhal Vijay* (1915).
26. Birendra Narayan, p. 79.
27. Jayanti Chattopaodhyaya, p. 227.

28. D.L. Roy enjoyed unparellelled popularity among the students. His plays used to be staged in the Hindu Hostel of Allahabad University every year on the eve of convocation. Sumitra Nandan Pant, famous Hindi poet, also used to act. Somnath Gupta, p. 125.
29. From a long list, mention can be made of *Shaligram Puni Vikram* (1906); Vrindavan Lal's *Senapati-Udal* (1909); Sukdev Narain Singh's *Veerasdav* (1909); Sudarseva's *Dayananda* (1917); Badrinath Bhatt's *Chandragupta* (1915), *Tulsidas* (1915) and *Durgawati* (1926); Prem Chand's *Karbala* (1924); Udai Shankar Bhatt's *Chandragupta Maurya* (1931) and *Vikramaditya* (1933); Baldev Misra's *Mirabai* (1919); Jayshankar Prasad's *Kalyani Parinay* (1912), *Rajyashri* (1915), *Vishakh* (1921), *Ajat Shatru* (1922), *Skandgupta* (1928), *Chandragupta* (1931), *Dhruvaswamini* (1933); Jagannath Prasad Milind's *Pratapa-Pratijna* (1928); Laxmi Dhar Vajpayee's *Raj Kumar Kuntal* and Govind Das's *Harsa* ((1935); Chandaraja Bhandari's *Siddharta Kumar* (1922) and *Samraat Ashoka* (1923) etc.
30. Jayanti Chattopadhyaya, p. 230.
31. "*Anumaan kiya gayaa hai ki Hindi mein jo naveen pustake prakaashit hoti hai unme 95 pratishat anuvaad hain. Mere ek mitra ne ek baar kaha tha—Hindi ke Prakashak Bangali sahitya par itne mughd ho rahe hai ki Bangali pustakon ke anuvaad ke bina aur koi pustak pasand hi hahin karte. Yadi tum inke paas koi maulik pustak bhej do to sambhav hai ki ve use chhapna swikaar na kare. Parantoo yeh asambhav hai ki yadi us par "bangala anuvaad" bhej do use saharsh pasand na kar liya jaye.*" Preface to Sudarshan's *Teerthyatra* (Ist ed.), 189, pp. 3-6. Qtd Taneja, p. 187.

    In the opinion of Premchand: "*Hindi me achhe dramon ki kami hai. D.L. Roy ke natakon ko nikaal dijiye to hamare paas kuch bhi nahin reh jaata.*" (Preface to Ugra's Mahatma Isa). Sudarsana in preface to his *Anjana* (1922) again portrayed the pathetic scene of Hindi drama in these words: "*Is samay tak Hindi me jo uttam natak chhape hain, ve praaya*

Bangla ya Angrezi natakon ka anuvaad hai. Hindi me maulik natakon ka atishaya abhaav hai. Mujhe kam se kam itna santosh hai ki maine maulik natak me ek vradhi ki hai."

32. Jayanti Chattopadhyaya has shown her scepticism, p. 226.
33. *Loc. cit.*
34. *Ibid.*, p. 231.
35. Lakshmi Narayan Misra, Introduction to *Mukti ka Rahasya* (4th ed.), pp. 19-21.
36. Sahitya Sandesh, "*Hindi Natkkar apni apni kalam se,*" *Natak ank*, p. 97.

Prasad and Bengali Literature

Prasad was unequivocally influenced by the Bengali literary figures like Michael Madhusuadan Dutt, D.L. Roy and Rabinranath Tagore. The point, however, is how did he come to know about the Bengali literature? Perhaps he went through the Hindi renderings of the Bengali works, a corpus of which had already accumulated in his creative period. While not discounting such a possibility, the fact is that he himself knew Bengali and so had direct access to literary works of his choice and interest. His knowledge of Bengali seems to be quite sound—a fact to which Nathu Ram Premi, who translated D.L. Roy's plays in Hindi, testifies in these words: "*Anth me kaashi ke Sahridyra sukavi Babu Jayshankar Prasad ko dhanyavaad dena ham apna kartavya samajte hain, jinhone is [Rana Pratap Singh] natak ke geeton ka sundar anoovad kar dene ki kripa ki.*"[1]

Not only did he closely read Bengali literature but was also not hesitant to borrow literally from it. His poetry, for example, unmistakably bears the stamp of Rabindranath Tagore and Michael Madhusudan Dutt. His introduction of blank verse in *Karunalaya* (1912) testifies to Michael Madhusudan Dutt's influence. The *Chhayvaad* movement of which he was one of the exponents emerged under the impetus of Rabindranath Tagore. He read Tagore and D.L. Roy deeply, and widely.[2] The publication of English edition of *Gitanjali* in 1911 stirred many a creative mind in Indian literature, Prasad being one of them. Under Tagore's spell, he wrote prose lyrics and subsequently wove them into his novels, short stories, dramas and poetry. *Kanan Kusum* (1912), his poetic work, has been written in the aftermath of *Gitanjali*. A reading of his early poems would show how deeply he was influenced by Tagore: Tagore's poem, "*Ekati namaskare/Prabhuekti namaskare*." Prasad came out with "*Jis mandir ka dwar sada unmukta raha hai/Jis mandir me ek naresh samaan raha hai. . . . Namasker mera sada/poore vishwa grahst ko*"; following *Gitanjali*'s "*Jeevan Jaakhan shukaijaad/karuna dhaaraain eiso*." Prasad reproduced it in his poem "*Jab Pralaya ka ho samay jwalamukhi mukh khol de. . . . Tab bri prabo! Yeh man khiche tabi predhaara paash me*" (*Indu*, February 1914). As a matter of fact, there are a number of poems in *Kanan Kusum* and *Jharna* (1927) which bear the stamp of *Gitanjali*. He has faithfully reproduced Tagore's ideas in his poems. *Gitanjali*'s eleventh poem has stirred him to write two poems: "*Jab maante hain vyapi jal bhoomi mein, anil mein/Tara shasaank mein bhi aakash mein atal mein/phir kyo ye hat hain pyare mandir mein weh nahin hai/Yes shabd jo nahin hai uske liye nahin hain*," and under the title *Aadesh*, "*Prarthna aur tapasya kyo?/Pujari kiski hai yeh bhakti/ Dara hain tu hij paapon se/Isi se karta nij apmaan/dukhi par karuna chhan bhar ho/ Prarthna pehron ke badle/hame vishwas hai ki weh satya/ karega aakar tab sammaan*."[3]

On his prose narrative, the influence of Bengali literature is also discernible. For instance, a number of his short stories have been modelled after Tagore. For instance, *Pratima* has been written after *Gitanjali*'s *Bhagn mandir ke devata*; his story *Madan Mrinalani* portrays the life of the Brahmo Samaji Bengali family. Similar is the case with many stories in *Pratidhwani*. His novel *Titli* (1934) bears the tinge of Tagore's novels. As a playwright, he was affected by D.L. Roy. *Kalyani Parinay* (1912) was written by him after D.L. Roy's publications of *Chandragupta*. It is through D.L. Roy that he acquired technique of western dramaturgy. The text of his plays shows a close relationship with D.L. Roy. For instance, compare these passages: "*Chhamaa manushya ka dharma hai—kewal Brahman ka nahin. Chhamaa karne se jo athah sukh hai us par kya akeyle Brahman ka hi adhikaar hai*" (Roy's *Chandragupta*, 3.6): "*Chhamaa par manushya ka adhikaar hai, weh pashu ke paas nahin miltee. Pratihinsa paashav dharm hai. Utho, main tumhe chhamma karti hoon.*" (Prasad's *Skandgupta*, Act 2). "*Matragupta—Amrit ke sarovar me swarn kamal khil raha tha. Saurabh aur paraag ki chehel pehel thi. Savere Surya ki kirnen use choomne ko laut-ti thi. Sandhya me sheetal chandni use apni chaadar se dhak aeti thi. Us madhur saundarya, us ateendrya jagat ki saakaar kalpana ki aur maine haath barhayaa tha. Wahi swapn toot gaya*" (Prasad's *Skandgupta*, 1.3) and "*Sikander: Sachmuch Selucus! Kitna vichitra hai yeh desh? Din mein prachand surya iske pragaat neel aakash ko poorn kar deta hai aur raatri mein shubhra chandrma aakar use jyotsna se snaan karaata hai*" (Roy's *Chandragupta*, 1.1). Similar passages can be quoted in plenty from both the *Chandraguptas*.

The contribution of Bengali literature in transmitting western influence to Hindi has been acknowledged universally by the Hindi literati, yet, the intriguing fact is that nowhere does Prasad deem it worth mentioning. For example, while in his essay on 'Rangmanch'[4] or 'Drama' he has referred to Shakespeare, Shaw and Ibsen—he also says about taking inspiration from the West—but has maintained a studied silence on the Bengali model which he and his predecessors looked for inspiration and guidance.

NOTES

1. "*Nathu Ram Premi ke Shabd*," *Rana Pratap Singh* (5th edn). Sam. 1978, p. 12. Qtd. Govind Chatak, p. 47.
2. Ram Ratan Bhatnagar, *Prasad aur unka Sahitya*, p. 21.
3. Qtd. Ram Ratan Bhatnagar, pp. 80-82.
4. Jayshankar Prasad, *Kavya aur kala tatha anya Nibandh*.

Role of Bengali Literature as a Mediator of Western Influence and Hindi

The contemporary literary genres in Hindi began under the influence of the West. The influence of the West first flowed through the fields of Bengal[1] and "breathed life into the dormant spirit of Bengali literature." From Bengal, it came to Hindi, thanks to the foresightedness and painstaking efforts of Bhartendu and Acharya Mahavir Prasad Dwivedi.[2] That Bengal model provided real impetus and guidance to the creative minds in Hindi to assimilate western influence is an incontrovertible fact.[3]

This has taken place despite the fact that the general mode of a foreign writer's 'reception' and 'influence' is through the conduit of his rendering into Hindi—or for that matter—in any other Indian language. Take for instance Shakespeare's influence on Prasad's drama.

By the time Prasad emerged on the scene there were a number of Hindi translations of Western, in particular Shakespeare's, works. Munshi Imadaad Ali's translation of *The Comedy of Errors* in 1879 was the first of its kind and since then, about 200 translations/adaptations of Shakespeare have been brought out,[4] although faithfulness of many of these translations is questionable.

According to some Hindi scholars—Visvanth Misra,[5] J.P. Misra,[6] Sripati Sharma[7] and D.K. Lal Srivastva[8]—the Western influence in Prasad's drama is too obvious. For instance, his *Prayashchita* (1914) is based on Shakespeare's *Macbeth*; *Rajyashri* (1915) echoes *Henry IV, Part II*; in

Vishakh (1921) various details are worked out under the influence of Shakespeare's *Measure for Measure*, besides its inspiration from *Richard II*, *Richard III* and *Hamlet*; *Ajatshatru* (1922) was influenced by *King Lear*, whereas some of its characters bear the stamp of characters in *Richard II*; *Janmejaya Ka Nagyajna* recalls Shakespeare's *Macbeth*, *Hamlet* and other plays; *Kamna* (1923-24) incorporates the use of pathetic fallacy from *King Lear*; *Skandgupta Vikaramditya* (1928) shows influence of *Hamlet*, while in matters of action and conflict, chance or accident it is said to have been inspired from *King Lear*, *Macbeth*, *Othello* and *Romeo and Juliet*; in *Chandragupta*, in devising external conflict, Prasad is said to have been indebted to Shakespeare's *Titus Andronicus*.

Hindi scholars have questioned such attempts as far-fetched: "*Yeh ghoshnaye theek usi prakaar ki hai jaise yeh kaha jaye ki England aur Denmark ke itihas ne Magadh ke itihas ko prabhavit kiya hai.*"[9] (These declarations fit in the same pattern as if it were claimed that history of Magadh has been influenced by the history of England and Denmark.) But the point is: was influence of Shakespeare imbibed by Prasad directly or through Hindi renderings or through Bengali works of D.L. Roy?

The Hindi scholars seem to be unanimous that it is through Bengali works, particularly D.L. Roy, that Shakespeare's influence permeated to Hindi: "*Prasad tuk hamaare liye Bengal hi 'Paschim' tha, parantoo is paschim ko bhi hamne apne parivesh ke anuroop grahan kiya. Prasad ke baad Paschim ka seedha prabhav shuru to hua par Hindi natak ne Bharatiya dharatal na chhora.*" [10] (Upto Prasad, Bengal was "West" for us. However, we did not copy it blindly, rather this 'Western model' was rooted in our native soil. After Prasad, the influence of the West came direct but Hindi drama did not give up its Indian base).

NOTES

1. According to Sushil Kumar De, "'The literary history of Bengal in the 19th century is really the history of influence of European on Bengali thought," *Bengali Literature in the Nineteen Century*, p. 55. The Bengali intelligentsia, however, used this influence creatively, realizing that "No mere foreign grafting can ever thrive and flourish, unless the tender plant on which the grafting is to be made first germinates and sends its roots deep into its own indigenous soil when the living free in thus nourished and watered by foreign manure may add flavour and beauty to it." Qtd. Priyaranjan Sen, *Western Influence in Bengali Literature*, p. 276.
2. Dwivedi wrote an article in 1903 in *Saraswati* in which he exhorted Hindi creative minds to learn (and not imitate) from Michael's example of introducing alien forms of expression like blank verse: "*Madhusudan ke samya tak Bangla ke amitakshar chhand nahin likhe jaate thei. . . . Logon ka yeh anumaan tha ki Bangla mein amitakshar chhand ho hi nahin sakte. Is baat ko Michael ne nirmool siddh kar diya. . . . Jab is prakar ke chhand Bangla mein likhe ja sakte hain aur bari yogyta se likhe ja sakte hain, tab unka Hindi mein bhi likha jaana sambhav hai. Likhne wala achhaa aur yogya hona chahiye.*" Qtd. Ram Vilas Sharma, *Mahavir Prasad Dwivedi aur Hindi Nav Jagaran*, p. 313.
3. Take for instance, the case of the introduction of the genre of 'novel in Hindi.' Acharya Ram Chandra Shukla has acknowledged the fact that the void in Hindi could be filled by turning to Bengal, rather direct to the West, "*Sahitya ke is vibhag ki shoonyta sheeghr hatane ke liye unke (Bangla) anuvaad avashyak pratit huye.*" Qtd. Ram Chandra Shukla, *Hindi Sahitya Itihas*, p. 446.

4. Some of the Hindi renderings of Shakespeare's plays are: *Love's Labour Lost—Nishfal Prem* (trans. Ganga Prasad, 1914); *Comedy of Errors—Bhramjaalak* (trans. Munshi Ratan Chand Sahib, 1882); *Merchant of Venice—Venice Nagar Ka Vyapaari* (trans. Munshi Ratan Chand Sahib, 1979); *Venice Ka Saudagar* (trans. Thakur Dayal Singh, 1885); *Venice ka Baanka* (trans. Gokul Chand Sharma, 1888); *Merry Wives of Windsor—Windsor ki Hansmukh Striyaa* (trans. Ganga Prasad, 1914); *Much Ado about Nothing—Vyarth Haura Machana tha* (trans. Kashi Nath Khatri, 1884); *As You Like It—Jaisa tumhe Pasand aawe karo* (trans. Kashinath Khatri, 1884); *Jaisi Jaaki* (trans. Jai Vijai Narain Singh Sharma. 1912); *Winter's Tale—Sharad Ritu ki Kahani* (trans. Kashinath Khatri, 1882) and (trans. Ganga Prasad, 1922); *Jaaron Ki Kahani* (trans. Jai Vijai Narain Singh Sharma, 1922); *Titus Andronicus* (trans. Ganga Prasad, 1914); *Romeo and Juliet—Prem Lila* (trans. Gopinath Purohit, 1896); *King Lear—Sneh Pariksha* (trans. Badrinarain, 1903); *Macbeth* (trans. Visnu Sharma); *Antony and Cleopatra* (trans. Ganga Prasad, 1914) etc.
5. See V.N. Misra, *Hindi Natak Par Paschatya Prabhav* (Allahabad, 1966).
6. J.P. Sharma, *Shakespeare's Impact on Hindi Literature* (New Delhi: Munshiram Manohar Lal, 1970).
7. Sripati Sharma, *Hindi Natakon par Paschatya Prabhav* (1961).
8. D.K. Lal Srivastava, *The Influence of Western on Modern Hindi Drama*.
9. Govind Chatak, *Prasad Ke Natak: Swaroop aur Sanrachana* (Delhi: Sahitya Bharti, 1975), pp. 47-48.
10. Satyendra Taneja, *Hindi Natak: Punarmulyaankan* (Kanpur: Grantham), p. 333.

Plot

Prasad wrote *Chandragupta* on the basis of his meticulous research of history of the Mauryan empire to trace the social lineage of Chandragupta. According to his findings Chandragupta Maurya belonged to a *Kshatriya* lineage, whereas his predecessors, Vishakhadatta and D.L Roy have shown him of a lowly birth. Nevertheless, the theme of the drama is focussed upon Chanakya and Chandragupta.

Prasad's play depicts three main events: the invasion of Alexander; the downfall of the Nand dynasty and the defeat of Selucus. The play thus covers the incidents of a span of 23 years (BC 327-305) and the events take place at various places spread from Kusumpur (Magadh) to Gandhar, Panchnand and Malva; from street to palace, from courtroom to prison-cell, from forest to river bank, thus providing ample scope for spectacle ana stage-craft.

The plot has been taken from history but the playwright has introduced sub-plots which are the creation of his own imagination to subserve the purpose of his artistry. The sub-plots are mainly connected with love affairs between Chandragupta and Cornelia (daughter of Selucus); Chandragupta and Malvika, Chandragupta and Kalyani: Philips and Cornelia, Simharan and Alka; Rakshas and Suvasini; Parvateshwar and Kalyani and Chanakya and Suvasini.

Structurally, the play is divided into four acts—apparently not in conformity with Shakespearean technique—and 44 scenes. The distribution of the scenes across the acts d 44 scenes. The distribution of the scenes across the acts is uneven: The first act has 11, second 10, third 9 and fourth 14.

There are twenty-seven characters, eighteen male and 9 female, supported by a host of others for crowd effects. Among the female characters, three are lovers of Chandragupta—Cornelia, Kalyani and Malvika. Both Kalyani and Malvika are made to leave for good in the mid-stream and the way the playwright has accomplished the task, does not depict him in favourable light. The question arises: why did he feel the necessity to create these characters at all? In my opinion, the reason was Roy's Chanakya—a shattered and broken-hearted person after his wife's death and daughter's kidnapping. Prasad also wanted his Chanakya with a throbbing heart and Roy's Chanakya did not suit him due to his own tragedy.[2] Had he decided to present Roy's Chanakya as such, it might have been beyond his emotive control.

As a matter of fact, Prasad has rather been rapacious in depicting events covering a span of quarter of century in comparison to his predecessors. For instance, *Mudrarakshas* begins after the fall of Nand and Chanakya's personal wrong had been avenged. The objective of the play is to show how Chanakya takes measures to strengthen Chandragupta's rule and foiling the designs of his opponent Rakshas, "Ah! who is he who that desires to attack Chandragupta when I am alive?" The events cover a period of about a year and no female appears among the *dramatis personae.* Roy's play is divided into five acts on the pattern of Shakespeare and covers the last two events of Prasad's drama. It has, in all, 12 characters; 9 male and 3 female.

II

The play opens with a scene from Taxila where Chanakya is a teacher and Chandragupta and Simharan, the crown prince of Malav, are students. In the same scene the crown prince of Gandhar, Ambhik and his sister Alka are also introduced.

The first scene depicts the political scenario prior to the invasion of Alexander: the ruler of Gandhar had turned quisling in his rivalry with the ruler of Panchnand, Poru (Parvateshwar); the threat to national unity and defence looming large on the minds of the patriots—Chanakya and the alumnus of Taxila.

The drama inaugurates with a dialogue between Chanakya and Simharan discussing the implications of the unholy alliance of the ruler of Gandhar with Alexander. Ambhik is indignant to hear this and this leads to acrimonious exchanges between them. Alka, shocked over her brother's outrageous behaviour, is enamoured of Simharan and his cause. She also entreats him to leave Gandhar for reasons of his safety.

However, more than anyone else, it is Chanakya who perceives the gravity of situation and puts forth his apprehensions to Chandragupta, "*Panchnand Parvateshwar ke virodh ke karan yahan shudra hridya Ambhik yavno ka swaagat karega aur Arya-vratta ka naash hoga.*" (1.1. p. 51) (Due to his opposition of Parvateshwar, (the ruler of) Panchnand, this ignoble Ambhik would throw red carpet to the infidels and that would mean an end of Aryavratta). It is here that Chandragupta assures him "*Gurudev, vishwas rakhiye, yeh sab kuch nahi hone payega, yeh Chandragupta aapke charno ki shapath purvak pratiggya karta hai ki Yavan yahan kuch na kar sakenge.*" (1.1.51) (My esteemed teacher, rest assured that nothing of the sort would be allowed to materialize. This Chandragupta takes this solemn vow that the infidels will never be able to succeed in their designs).

By highlighting such contours of conflicts the playwright has set the background of the Greek invasion as well as his hinting at its logical outcome.

The next scene takes us to Kusumpur (Magadh) showing king Nand's revelry with courtesan Suvasini entertaining him by her dance. Dramatically, the scene depicts the affluence of Magadh and its carefree atmosphere. Rakshas, who is an accomplished artist, has pleased Nand. He, being a highly accomplished musician, is appointed a minister. The third scene is focussed on Chanakya when he returns to Kusumpur and finds his father's dwelling in utter ruins in the aftermath of his arrest and detention for his defiance to Nand's autocracy. To his dismay, Suvasini becomes Nand's courtesan. Chanakya's pulling out the pillar, which acted as a support to his father's hut, shows not merely his anguish and despondency but through this, he also wipes out the past and underlines his resolve to build the future.

Set in Kusumpur, the next scene shows Suvasini, offended by Chanakya, gravitating towards Rakshas all the more. Kalyani, the princess of Magadh, is miraculously rescued from a leopard by Chandragupta, and she, in turn, is attracted towards him. The scene arouses curiosity about the possibilities of Suvasini-Rakshas-Chanakya forming a love triangle and the result of Kalyani's attachment to Chandragputa. The scene, nevertheless, provides a movement to the plot. The fifth scene relates to the court of king Nand. It shows Nand's estrangement with Parvateshwar for his refusal to enter into wedlock with Nand's daughter due to his Buddhist *Shudra* status. Besides, when Chanakya tries to bring home to Nand the need to resist the Greek invaders in unison with Parvateshwar, he is subjected to humiliation and thrown out of the court. It is here that Chanakya swears to wreck vengeance by keeping his string of head's hair unbound until Nand's extinction. Chanakya is put behind the bars.

The next scene reverts to the banks of Indus where Malvika, the princess of Sindhudesh, wants to deliver a strategic plan to Alka and a Greek soldier tries to snatch it. What a coincidence that Simharan appears on the scene at that very juncture and intervenes and in the process gets wounded. The soldier flees in desperation. Alka is imprisoned and is taken to the King of Gandhar who sets her free, handing over his realm to Ambhik.

The seventh scene shows brooding Chanakya lodged in jail along with Katyayan but again a feat by Chandragupta. He breaks the gate of the prison-cell, kills the guard, terrorises Rakshas and frees Chanakya single-handedly.

After coming out of jail Chanakya made a dash to Parvateshwar (sc. 9) in order to convince him to make a common cause with Chandragupta in order to overthrow the corrupt regime of Nand. He also removes Parvateshwar's doubt about Chandragupta's *Kshatriya* lineage and things come to such a pass that Parvateshwar deports Chanakya.

In the next scene, Alka encounters Selucus in the forest. Through a co-incidence, Chanakya and Chandragupta are also passing through and thus Selucus's designs are foiled. In turn, Chandragupta faints, Chanakya fetches water and it is just then that a tiger comes and before it could harm Chandragupta, Selucus kills it. Strangely, Chandragupta could know about it only after he regained consciousness. He feels grateful to Selucus for this act.

In the last scene of the first Act, the contending personages—Chanakya Chandragupta and Alka, on the one side,

Alexander and his lieutenants on the other are face to face with each other at the *ashram* of sage Dandayan. The playwright has utilized the sage to impress the Greeks (West) to learn from India's past. Dandayan tries to bring home to Alexander—through his discourse as well as his example of leading a life of mortification and self-abnegation—the ideals of love, peace and universal brotherhood. To a question from Alexander, his reply was "*Tumhey Sadbudhi miley*" (1.11) (May wisdom dawn upon you) and what he said to Alexander at the end was prophecy about Chandragupta which startled everybody, "*Alexander, Saavdhan! (Chandragupta ko dikhakar) dekho yeh Bharat ka bhaavi Samrat tumhare samney betha hai*" (Beware Alexander! (Pointing to Chandragupta) Look! In front of you sits the future Emperor of India). Selucus' daughter Cornelia and Chandragupta see each other in distraction.

In retrospect, the first act captures the political situation prior to the Greek invasion, alignment of the forces and provides a hint for the future developments. The subject matter has been woven around Chandragupta: he is everywhere, has relations with everybody from Chanakya, Simharan to Alexander, Selucus, Cornelia to Alka/Malvika/Kalyani and Parvateshwar to Ambhik, Nand and Rakshas.

Viewing from the point of structural cohesiveness, the number of scenes could have been minimized by either deleting some scenes viz. 2, 3, 4 or incorporating the material into others.[3]

The impact of the Bengali play is quite discernible. For instance, Chandragupta's vow before Chanakya (1.1.51) echoes Roy's (1.4.32); Chanakya's soliloquy in the prison-cell is reminiscent of his monologue in Roy (1.2. p. 14). The circumstances and the manner in which Chanakya was stormed out of Nand's court is akin to Roy's.[4] The idea of the figure of Dandayan as well as his discourse seems to have been borrowed from Helen's description of one Pandit Deyojenis (3.4. p. 76); the sage's prophecy about Chandragupta is the same as was made by Alexander in Roy's play (1.1.14); the modus operandi of introducing Cornelia with Helen to Chandragupta is the same: Helen is charmed by Chandragupta's valour in combating Antigonus but does not utter a single word (Roy's *Chandragupta,* 1.1. p. 13) and here in Prasad, Cornelia is enamoured in her first glance after Dandayan's prophetic utterances but keeps mum. The story comes to a full circle in Act 2.1 when she says to herself: "*Ek ghatna ho gayee kintoo us ghatna se kisi aur ka bhi sambandh hai, usay kaise bhul jaun weh bhi ah! kitna akarshak hai. Kitna tarang sankul hai. Isi Chandragupta ke liye na us sadhu ne Bhavishyawani ki hai, Bhawi Samraat hone ki. Usme kitni vinaysheel veerta hai*" (Prasad's *Chandragupta,* 2.1. p. 91).[5]

Act II, concentrating upon North-West, builds up the tension in the play through a series of events involving Chandragupta and Selucus against Philips, Ambhik/Philips/Anesacretes collectively making an attempt on Chandragupta's life following Alexander's order to arrest him: Chanakya's scheming against Parvateshwar consequent upon which he disguised as celibate, Chandragputa as snake-charmer and Alka-Simharan as acrobats infiltrate into his army camp; Kalyani joining Parvateshwar from Magadh in the guise of man; fierce battle between Alexander and Parvateshwar; Parvateshwar-Alka-Simharan triangle of love and above all Alexander and Selucus getting seriously wounded and besieged by Simharan and Chandragupta. The Act begins at dawn on the bank of Indus: a museful Helen looking the Indian side of the river. She gives vent to her feelings both in prose and verse extolling India and her cultural heritage. Philips, the Greek soldier and her lover, makes advances towards her but Chandragupta intervenes and foils his designs. As a result, Helen and Chandragupta are mutually enchanted and this creates a reaction in Philips. Feeling offended, he harbours grudge against both, but more against Chandragupta. An injured Philips is desperate to wreak vengeance: he provokes Selucus and enters into league with Ambhik/ Ancesacretes. The scene introduces Alexander who asks for Chandragupta's help against Magadh. Not only does Chandragupta decline the request of the Greeks but prepares his plans to put an end to the Greek design. An indignant Alexander orders his detention but Chandragupta gets away wounding the trio of Ambhik/Philips/ Anesacretes.

Chanakya and others sneak into the army camp of Parvateshwar and are detained in the mistaken identity of their being spies of the enemy. In the battle between Alexander and Parvateshwar, Chandragupta commands the troops brought by Kalyani from Magadh. Parvateshwar is defeated and falls in the hands of the Greeks. It is here that the famous dialogue between Alexander and Parvateshwar has been reproduced:

Sikander: Vir Parvateshwar! Ab main tumhare saath kaisa vyavhar karoon? Parvateshwar: Jaisa ki ek nripati anay nripati ke sath karta hai.

Overwhelmed by Parvateshwar's valour, not only does Alexander release him, but also makes peace with him. Simharan who is wounded in the battle is imprisoned by Ambhik along with Alka.

Chanakya has taken full advantage of their detention. He asks Alka to express her desire before Parvateshwar to become his empress not earnestly but just to hoodwink him.

The device works well and Parvateshwar reposes his full confidence in her. It is through Parvateshwar that Alka comes to know about Alexander's message for him to reach on the bank of Ravi with his cavalry in Operation Malva. Alka overwhelms Parvateshwar and brings about release of Simharan.

The next scene shows war preparations in Malva and Simharan and Chandragupta spurning Alexander's request to meet him. In the following scene Chanakya tactfully prevents both Rakshas and Kalyani from leaving for Magadh. All these developments culminate into fierce fight between the Greek and Malav in which even the womenfolk resist the Greek onslaught. Alexander is seriously wounded and Selucus besieged. Chandrqgputa, however, lets him off as a mark of respect and thus, Chardragupta emerges victorious proving his intrepidity and valour.

The Act, an entity in itself, has been stretched into 10 scenes due to playwright's penchant for sub-plots. However, apart from showing the brighter side of both Chanakya and Chandragupta, the sub-plots rather hamper the momentum. Quite a number of scenes, viz. 5, 6, 7 and 8, could be altogether dispensed with or reorganized after due bunching.[6]

The Act has echoes of the Bengali play. For instance, Cornelia's praise of India (2.1.79) is quite akin to Alexander's in Roy's play (1.1. pp. 9-10). The only difference is that what Cornelia pronounces in the dawn, Roy's Alexander is doing the same in dusk. There is a close similarity between outrageous behaviour of Philips with Cornelia and their counterparts in Roy. In Prasad's play it was Chandragupta who saved her, in Bengali play it was Selucus. Philips (Anitgonus) turns out to be the rival of Chandragupta.

Act III depicts political developments in Magadh. And rightly so. Having inflicted decisive defeat upon the Greeks, the extinction of Nand's dynasty is the next agenda before Chanakya and Chandragupta. For accomplishing this task, Chanakya has employed all the weapons in his arsenal: duplicity, intrigue, diplomacy and what not. The play, however, does not pick up tempo until the departure of the Greek from India (3.3).

The first item in Chanakya's scheme of things is to bring about estrangement between Rakshas and Nand which he does by resorting to tricks and intrigues. First, he conveys to Rakshas about Suvasini's arrest by Nand charged of hatching conspiracy with him. Then he enacts drama of his arrest and subsequent release (courtesy Chanakya) as well as informing him about Alka-Simharan wedding, Alexander, in person, blessing the couple. In the following scene Parvateshwar is shown feeling humiliated by Alexander's blessing and his being neglected. He is so exasperated that he attempts to commit suicide which was prevented by Chanakya. After their departure appear Cornelia and Chandragupta, both admiring each other. Nevertheless, Cornelia is also extolling India as "cradle of humanity" and what a chance that Philips appears on the scene and embarrasses her. But he is rebuffed by her while Chandragupta gives him a stern warning. Afterwards, Rakshas, Kalyani and Chanakya are seen together. Here Chanakya advises Kalyani to return to Magadh. Furthermore, he takes from Rakshas his ring on the pretext of conveying his message to Suvasini. In the third scene, Alexander leaves India and Chanakya commits Parvateshwar to lend his support to Chandragupta against Nand. Meanwhile, Rakshas also comes to know about Chanakya's duplicity and leaves for Magadh. In the same scene, Parvateshwar deputes Simharan as the top brass of his armed contingent and deploy it against Magadh. At the moment, Chandragupta, being held up, does not proceed to Magadh because of his duel due with Philips. The fifth scene shows Nand making an attempt on Suvasini's chastity which was, however, frustrated by the timely intervention of Rakshas. The next scene highlights Chanakya's trickery: Malvika, disguised as courtesan, is deputed to deliver a letter and the ring from Rakshas, ostensibly marked to Suvasini, to Nand and thereby simultaneously informing him about Rakshas' plan of wedding with her. It is in the same scene that Shaktar and Chanakya meet each other.

Malvika accomplishes the task. As expected, Nand is infuriated and he ordains to apprehend both of them—Suvasini and Rakshas. In the last two scenes the drama acquires tempo: Philips is killed by Chandragupta. He is heading towards Magadh with Simharan on constant vigil and Chanakya planning for the final show down with Nand. On the pattern of mass movement, people are roused and exhorted, to revolt against the misdeeds of Nand. The masses respond positively and seeing Rakshas in chains are shocked and infuriated. This provides another nail in the coffin. The masses are now led by Shaktar, Varruchi and Maurya, the sworn enemies of Nand and his victims. It is chaos all around, Nand himself is in the dock in the people's court. At this juncture, Chandragupta's appearance on the scene creates a catalytic effect. Nand is totally demoralized and is at his wits' end. Out of sheer desperation, he orders his security guards to arrest all the 'rebels.' While this happens in the palace, an attack is launched on the city as well. Nand is detained by Chandragupta. Subsequently, the final part of the drama—its culmination—takes place. Chanakya comes into his full form, taunts Nand for his misdeeds and exhibits his own hypocrisy. On the one hand, he delivers an inflammatory lecture inciting and provoking the masses to such a pitch that they cry out for Nand's blood and on the other, he appeals to them to forgive him. It is at this juncture that Shaktar fatally stabs Nand—which is in line with Roy's play. Chanakya's game, however, does not end here. He manipulates to install Chandragupta as the sovereign. In Magadh, under the new dispensation, fundamental rights of life and liberty are extended to the people.

The last act is not organically linked with the preceding acts and it has come under sharp criticism mainly on two counts. First, there is little sense in stretching the play following the culmination i.e. Nand's killing and coronation of Chandragupta. A gap of sixteen years separates the two events i.e. coronation of Chandragupta and the second attack of the Greeks[8] which is the concern of the fourth Act. A number of critics have favoured the bifurcation of this Act. Even the internal structure of the Act is not flawless. A number of scenes are either redundant or could be reorganized. The scenes which could altogether be deleted are 7 and 8, while scenes 10 and 11 could be integrated into one and to which some part from scene 12 could also be added.[9]

Be that as it may, it is in this Act that the process of elimination of characters who ostensibly outlived their utility starts. Parvateshwar and Kalyani are made to die in the first scene—the former killed by Kalyani for his outrageous behaviour towards her and in turn, she also committing suicide on her own perceiving that there is no charm in life. The next scene attempts to build up tension: Rakshas wanting to settle his scores with Chanakya whom he considers his rival in love with Suvasini.

The third scene depicts a conflict between parents of Chandragupta with Chanakya. In the same scene, Chanakya hints the next target: it is Malvika who he exhorts to die for the sake of saving the life of Chandragupta. The poor Malvika, a blind adorer of Chandragupta, has no ambition; "*Madhup kab ek kali ka hai*" (4.1.67) embraces death "*Jaayo Priyatam! Sukhi jeewan bitane ke liye aur mein rahti hoon chir dukhi jeewan ka anth karne ke liye*" (4.4.169). The story of Malvika is reminiscent of the story of Chhayaa with the exception that Roy has not been so cruel.

The next scene shows Chanakya in a remorseful mood. However, the reason is not Malvika, rather, it is his ego that has been hurt by Chandragupta and made him part company with him. This part of the story is also similar to Roy's play. Yet, not only does he stage a come back and shows his acumen but also mobilizes forces against the invasion of the Greek. Even Ambhik falls in line. Alka is the star campaigner mobilizing the masses to unitedly resist the Greek. There is an all-pervasive atmosphere of patriotism gripping the masses. But that is not all for Chanakya. He urges Suvasini to marry Rakshas, infiltrate into the Greek camp as a detenue and assess for herself Cornelia's reaction about her wedding with Chandragupta and finally to change Rakshas.

The next scene shows Cornelia admonishing Rakshas as a 'traitor' (exactly what Helen does). She also picks up a row with her father questioning his wisdom to launch invasion over India (it is also in line with her counterpart of Roy). The problems of Chandragupta are not over because Simharan and Chanakya still feel alienated. Nevertheless, he is not cowed down by the Greek threat. On the other hand, Suvasini manages to reach Cornelia and the discourse between the two throws light on Prasad's perception of status of married women in the world of 'Man.' This apart, Helen tries to dissuade her father reminding him of Chandragupta's act of gratitude to her in the wake of Philips' attempt to defile her. But it was of no consequence—there is a fierce battle. Chanakya organizes the show, Ambhik dying valiantly in harness and Selucus wounded seriously. The Greek camp is under siege. Rakshas escapes with Suvasini and Cornelia attempts to commit suicide which Chandragupta's timely intervention foils her bid. Selucus is defeated and is trapped on all sides. It is against this backdrop that he agrees to her daughter's marriage with Chandragupta.

The scene then reverts to Dandayan's hermitage. Rakshas, Suvasini Alka-Simharan, Chandragupta and his parents—all are there. Chandragupta's father makes a bid on Chanakya's life which Chandragupta condemns, and Chanakya shows his magnanimity and forgives him. Rakshas and Suvasini are married. Rakshas is appointed Chandragupta's minister at the behest of Chanakya.[10] The last scene is about the peace treaty. Chandragupta and Cornelia enter into wedlock, Chandragupta become the monarch of India and Cornelia, the glory of Greece, becomes the gracious empress. Chanakya renounces the world.

IV

Prasad's plot exhibits lack of structural unity. Due to spatio-temporal spread of the events, the plot becomes unwieldy. Even the internal structure of its separate acts lack cohesiveness and leaves much to be desired. This shows that Prasad is "not a good architect of plot."[11] The proliferation of sub-plots has not served any significant purpose except to express Prasad's views on a number of problems and highlight the brighter side of the protagonist. He has missed many opportunities and situations where he could have excelled in giving a dramatic turn. His creation of too many characters has ostensibly led him into a cul-de-sac which he solves by killing a good many of them. Nevertheless, much of his weaknesses have rather stemmed from his rapaciousness in incorporating historical material he painstaking collected.

There are incontrovertible evidences to show that Prasad, before writing his play, read Roy's and took liberally and abundantly from that and utilized in his construction of the plot. Yet, he has entwined his material through his technical garnishing with such finesse that one might not capture each and every part of his borrowing easily.

NOTES

1. According to Jaganath Sharma, the playwright wanted the drama to be spread in 5 Acts. *Prasad Ke Natakon Ka Shastriya Adhyayan*, p. 149.
2. Prasad himself was a broken-hearted person due to the demise of his two wives in quick succession.
3. Parmeswari Lal Gupta, *Prasad ke Natak*, p. 92.
4. In *Mudrarakshas*, this incident is not shown, because the play starts after Nand dynasty was brought down and his minister Rakshas, conspiring to depose Chandragupta. It is here that Chanakya hints at the incident: "What doomed man [person seeking his death] does not wish even now my tufted hair tied up! [The hair] which has been [destructive] black female-serpent [kaal-Sarpini] to the race of the Nandas, as which is [as though] the thick dark curling mass of smoke of the fire of my anger." Chanakya's soliloquy in Act 1, p. 21.
5. Mark her sentiments in Roy's Chandragupta: "Surya ast ho gayaa. Is drishya ko dekh kar aaj sindhu-tat ka weh garimamaya suryast yaad aa raha hai. . . . Magadh ka weh raajputra" (2.1, p. 30).
6. Parmeshwari Lal Gupta, p. 92.

7. The 'ring' story is taken from *Mudrarakshas*.
8. There is no incontrovertible evidence of the second attack by the Greeks. Nevertheless, it is a fact that "Chandragupta liberated north-western India from the thraldom of Selucus, who ruled over the area west of the Indus. In the war with the Greek Viceroy, Chandragupta seems to have come out victorious. Eventually peace was concluded between the two." R.S. Sharma, *Ancient India*, p. 86; Soviet Scholar K.A. Antonowa et. al in *A History of India*, p. 86, have opined that it was Chandragupta who in all likelihood attacked Selucus.
9. Parmeshwari Lal Gupta, p. 92.
10. The fate of Rakshas in the end is similar to *Mudrarakshas*.
11. Nagender, "Dramatic Art," *Jayshankar Prasad: His Mind and Art*, p. 157.

Characterization

Scholars have acclaimed *Chandragupta* as a "drama of character" in which the playwright has "built a splendid gallery of character-portraits which are unique creation of art. Each one of them, from the dominant figures to the casual characters, has a clear-cut identity. . . . Chanakya on the one hand and Malvika on the other."[1] The play has twenty-seven characters in all, eighteen male and nine females. These characters belong to two categories: historical and fictitious. The historical characters, in turn, can be classified into two types: real historical personages and those who have simply been referred to in history. The real historical personages are Chanakya, Chandragupta, Parvateshwar, Alexander, Selucus, Ambhik, Dandayan, Rakshas, Varruchi and Shaktar while Philips, Anescaretes, Sybretes, king of Gandhar, Kalyani and Cornelia belong to the second type. The fictitious characters—Simharan, Alka, Suvasini and Malvika—have been created by the playwright.

In *Mudrarakshas,* historical characters simply are three: Chanakya, Chandragupta and Rakshas, as against Chandragupta, Chanakya, Nand, Katayan, Alexander, Selucus, Antigonus (Philips), Helen (Cornelia) and Mura in the Bengali *Chandragupta.*

The *Mudrarakshas* is mainly concerned with Chandragupta's elevation to the throne of Magadha in the wake of the fall of the Nand dynasty, and the adoption of measures to strengthen his rule by Chanakya, the renowned politician of his time. Remarkably, the playwright has not indicated the concept of 'Indian nation.' D.L. Roy's play has covered mainly two events—extinction of Nand's dynasty and Chandragupta's elevation to the throne of Magadh in the wake of liquidation of Nand and triumph of Chanakya-Chandragupta over Selucus, the Greek invader, culminating into Chandragupta's marriage with his daughter and India emerging for the first time as a 'nation' under the reign of Chandragupta.

Prasad's drama has taken into account the events from Alexander's invasion, extinction of Nand dynasty and Chandragupta becoming the emperor of Indian nation after defeating Selucus. Prasad's main thrust has "been to show that Chandragupta and Chanakya were instrumental in creating a nationalist ethos in ancient India. D.L. Roy has shown Chanakya to install Chandragupta as the sovereign of the nation of Aryavratta.

It would, however, be in the fitness of things to point out the fallacy of the postulates of these playwrights, which they borrowed from the dominant intellectual discourse of their times, "they say that Chandragupta Maurya and Chanakya were nationalists because the stood up against the foreign (i.e. Greek) invaders in the north west and that there was a consciousness of an all-India entity called Jambudvipa or Bharatvarsha," observes Romila Thapar, "is to distort history." She goes on:

> There is no evidence that Chandragupta or Chanakya organized Indian kings against Alexander and the Greeks. The young Chandragupta's ambition was to capture the throne of Nanda king at Patliputra and he appears to have been uninterested in the Greeks. Towards the end of his reign, he made an amicable treaty with the Greek, Selucus Nicator ruling in Iran. . . . It does seem interesting that Chanakya should now

be projected as the conscience keeper of Indian nationalism, given that he had so little use for political morality. The Mauryan empire may have included almost the whole of the sub-continent but it lasted as such for barely a century and rapidly broke up into smaller kingdoms and states. This does not support the 'sublime nature of national culture' as well.[2]

II

Prasad belongs to *Chhayavaad* school, hence there is magic in his description. His characters are essentially human beings. Not only the ordinary but even his sublime characters look human and earthly on account of their susceptibility and inner conflict.

Prasad has been acclaimed for his exquisite portrayal of Chanakya, the key figure—rather the backbone—of his drama without whom its entire structure would collapse. The stereotype image of Chanakya is of a diehard, hot-headed Brahman—utterly heartless, fiendish, shrewd, of firm resolve and the master of statecraft like Machiavelli. Prasad's feat lies in the fact that he has invested Chanakya not only with the metaphysical values, but also with a pulsating human heart. On the one hand, Chanakya remains far away from cupidity and on the other, he is a human being. Yet, he never allows the surge of passions in him to overwhelm and bringing to naught his 'resolve to master this world.' It is this Chanakya who has been evaluated by the Hindi scholars as hands and shoulders above Roy's.

Prasad's Chanakya was a broken-hearted, shattered man ever since his childhood days: his father, Chanak, was deported by king Nand, his ancestral house was in utter ruins and, to cap it all, his beloved Suvasini had turned courtesan of Nand due to dire circumstances: "*Pita ka pata nahin, jhopri bhi na rahi, Suvasini abhinetri ho gayee—sumbhav hai peit ki jwala se. Ek saath do-do kutambon ka sarvnash*" (1.3, p. 59) (No clue of the whereabouts of father, the hut is in ruins, Suvasini has become actress—probably driven by the fire of belly. Simultaneous ruination of two families). Furthermore, "*Yeh saamne Kusumpur hai, jahan mere jeevan ka prabhat hua tha. Mere saral hridya mein utcrisht ichha thi ki koi bhi sundar man mera saathi ho. Pratyeik navin parichaya mein utsukta thi*" (Here is Kusumpur where I was born. I had pined for a companion of sweet disposition, wistfully looked to every new acquaintance and wished from the core of my heart to bestow all on her) (3.6 p. 142). But there was something else in store for him which he himself poignantly expresses in these words, "*Main avishwas, kootchakra aur chhalnao ka kankaal, kathortaon ka kendra. Ah! to is vishwa mein mera koi sahridya nahin? . . . Suvasini, na, na, na, yeh . . .*" (I—the skeleton of duplicity, intrigue and incredulity, the fountainhead of ruthlessness! Oh! Is there no darling for me in this world? Suvasini, no, no, no, she is none [for me]) (3.6 p. 142).[3]

It is quite natural for a lonely and shattered man like him to lose equanimity and falter in deep emotional moments. And this is what happened in his case, when he in his encounter with Suvasini lost control, albeit, for a moment. And here it was she who came to his rescue: "What is this Visnagupta; you have moral fibre to master this world, then why not yourself? And he is shaken, as if caught unawares "*Kya? Meri durbalta? Nahin!*" (What, my weakness? No!) (4.3 p. 165).[4] Quite poignant and touching indeed. And when Suvasini herself approached him, he is a changed man. To Suvasini's, "*Chanakya, tum itne nirdayee ho,*" (4.6. p. 180), his reply was, "*Suvasini. Weh swapn toot gaya. Is vijan baaluka . . . mein kankaal hoon*" (4.6. p. 180).[5]

The question, however, is, whether the idea of transplanting a human heart in heartless Chanakya is an origin of Prasad's mind? The answer is, 'No.' Rather, he has borrowed the idea from Roy. Roy's Chanakya also suffered blows of misfortune in his early childhood days; he was also a lonely person as the jaws of death had snatched his life partner and the dacoits kidnapped her sole daughter, the lone emotive support for him in his old days and what was worse was that the state did nothing to retrieve her.[7]

Clearly, both Chanakyas have the same aching in their hearts, one bleeding for her beloved and the other for his wife and daughter. As has been pointed out earlier, Prasad did not present Chanakya as identical to Roy's due to tragedy in his own life.

Be that as it may, politics was not Chanakya's ambition of life. Temperamentally, he was quite far away from it; "*Meri bhumi, meri vritti wahi mil jaye*; *main shastravyavsayi na rahoonga, main krishak banunga, mujhe rashtra ki bhalai se kya*" (If I could get my piece of land and my way of life restored, I would prefer to be a farmer than a priest. What have I to do with national interest?) (1.3. p. 59).

Yet, when he is driven by circumstances and has no option left, he plunges himself heart and soul into national politics. Unswayed by personal interest, he relentlessly, ruthlessly, using fair and foul means, "*Mahatvakanksha ka moti, nishthurta ki sipi mein rahta hai*" (4.1. p. 161),[8] keeps on working till he succeeds in changing history. He organizes the feuding satraps against the Greeks, installs Chandragupta as sovereign of Aryavratta by pulling down the tyrannical rule of Nand. Not only this, he also finds a solution to the lasting peace between Greece and India: he solemnizes Chandragupta's marriage with Selucus's daughter. But he reaches the pinnacle of glory when in the twilight of his life he renounces this world: "*Unhone virakt hokar shantimaya jeevan bitane ka nishchaya kiya hai*" (4.14. p. 203); "*Main chir-vishram ke liye sansaar se alag hona chahata hoon*" (4.14. p. 203); "*Main aaj nishkam ho raha hoon . . . ab mujhe apne antarnihit brahmanatva ki uplabdhi ho rahi hai*" (4.13. p. 199).

Nevertheless, when he takes a stock of his past, he is remorseful: there is inner conflict in him, "*Main Brahman hoon. Mera samrajya karuna ka tha. Baudhik dharm vinod karm tha. Santosh dhan tha . . . [main] kahan aa gaya. Mera jeevan rajnitik kuchakron aur kalankit ho utha hai. Kisi chhaya chitra, kisi kalpanik mahatvva ke peeche bhrampoorn anusandhan karta daur raha hoon. Shanti kho gayee, swarup vismrit ho gaya*" (4.4. p. 171) (I am a Brahman. Compassion was my kingdom, love my religion, contentment my wealth . . . where have I landed myself. . . . Political intrigues have heaped reproaches and blemish upon me. I am groping after will o' the wisp, looking for illusory goals. In pursuit of truth, I am off the track).

This again reminds us of Roy's Chanakya who feels sorry for his acts: "*Kintoo ek mahaan, pavitra ujwal rajya ko chhorkar main kahan ja raha hoon. Ab bhi uske aalok mandit shikhar main dekh raha hoon. Tab sab kuch andhkarachhan ho jane ke pahle hi main kyon na laut chaloon*" (4.1 p. 91).

In fact, both Chanakyas are prototypes of each other, albeit, Prasad has administered a little more dose of Brahmanism in his creation. But that does not bring about any basic change in their world-view, style and functioning, state of inner conflict, ruthlessness, egocentrism or commitment to install Chandragupta as the emperor of a united Aryavratta. Once the aim is achieved, Roy's Chanakya like

Prasad's demits his office and departs from the scene for good, "*Mera karya samaapta ho gaya. Ab main vida leta hoon . . . to aao Ma, mere jeevan ki godhuli mein poorn jyotsna ke aalok ke samaan aakar mere gadh aakaash ko vyapta kar do. Ma jag dhatri ke samaan mere jeern-mandir mein pravesh karke mera haath pakar lo, aur mujhe aalokit parkaal mein le chalo.*" (5.5. p. 130)

Some Hindi scholars have made a fetish about the magnanimity of Prasad's Chanakya vis à vis Roy's. For instance, Ojha[9] makes out that Prasad's Chanakya is far more humane because he dissuades the masses to condone Nand for his misdeeds and spare his life, whereas Roy's Chanakya instigates Katyayan to murder Nand. Ojha has adduced another proof of cruel nature of Roy's Chanakya—immersion of his tuft of hair in Nand's blood. However, Ojha has not placed the whole incident in perspective. Prasad's Chanakya resorts to sheer demagogy, denouncing Nand by cataloguing his crimes but he stirs public passions to such a pitch that cries of "*Vadh karo, hatya karo*" (kill him, murder him) fill the air.[10] Besides this, Ojha overlooks Chanakya's diabolic acts—of forcing Kalyani to commit suicide and his subsequent glee: "*Chandragupta, Aaj tum nishkantak huye*" (4.1. p. 161). Even Chandragupta is stunned over such a remark, "*Gurudev! Itni krurta!*" Clearly, both the Chanakyas are ruthless to the same degree in their objectives and to depict Prasad's Chanakya in favourable light, as Ojha does, is palpably biased and misplaced.

A striking similarity between the two Chanakyas is to be seen in their vision of a united India under the sway of Brahmanism: "*Brahman raaj karna nahin jaanta, raaj karna bhi nahin chahata. Haan, weh raajaon ka niyaman jaanta hai*" (3.2. p. 128) (Brahman is not skilful in statecraft, nor is he interested in it. Yes. he knows how to control the monarchs, how to make monarchs); "*Rashtra ka shubhchintan kewal Brahman hi kar sakta hai*" (1.5. p. 65). He will not allow any slackness in the rigidity of *Varna-ashram* system, "*Tere poshak vaish, sevak, shudra aur rakshak kshatriya hain*" (1.9 p. 81). Same is the view of Roy's Chanakya.[11] Clearly, both the Chanakyas have not only identical ideology but also articulate their feelings and reactions more or less in the same way.

Prasad's characterization of Chandragupta has also been singled out by scholars as a testimony to his workmanship.[12] Prasad's Chandragupta, in the opinion of some critics, has emerged qualitatively different from Roy's: "While Roy's *Chandragupta* was only a politician and a warrior, Prasad's *Chandragupta* is a character whose facets present a kaleidoscopic pattern."[13] What is, however, *sine qua non* for comparing any two characters is that they are placed in identical ambience and circumstances.

Chanakya is his saviour and philosopher-guide; his devotion to him is total: *"Yeh Chandragupta aapke (Chanakya) ke charnon ki shapathpurvak pratigya karta hai ki Yavan yahan kuch na kar sakenge"* (1.1 p. 50).

Roy's Chandragupta venerates Chanakya to the same degree, *"Gurudev . . . Mujhe kewal itna kahiye ki Chandragupta, tu aage badh . . . mujhe aur kuch nahin chahiye. Aur sab main kar loonga . . . (Charnon ke per chhookar)—shapath karta hoon Gurudev aap mujhe diksha dijiye*" (1.4. p. 32).

Both of them follow Chanakya unswervingly and unflinchingly. Prasad's Chandragupta cannot protest even in such a situation when he, in his heart of heart was convinced about Chanakya's wrongful act. For instance, he could not muster courage to censor Chanakya for the uncharitable remark he made on Kalyani's suicide.

But when the contradiction emerged between Chanakya and his father over the cancellation of victory festival, the situation becomes unbearable for him. It is here that he realizes, "*Meri satta ek katputli si hai . . . yeh partantrata kab tak chalegi*" (4.5. p. 170). And now he does not hesitate to assert his authority: "*Yeh achurn adhikar aap kaise bhog rahe hain? Kewal saamrajya ka hi nahin, dekhta hoon aap mere kutumb ka bhi niyantran apne haath mein lena chahate hain*" (4.4. p. 171). He shows the same self-confidence when Chanakya leaves out of disgust, "*Jaane do . . . to kya main asmarth hoon, uh! sab ho jayega*" (4.4 p. 171).[14]

And when the dust is settled, the same Chandragupta expresses his gratitude to Chanakya, "Gurudev ne yahan bhi mera dhyan nahin chhora, main unka apradhi hoon, Simharan" (4.10. p. 193). He rather disapproves of his father's attempt on Chanakya's life, "*aur apne Gurudev ka—is Arya saamrajya ke nirmaankarta Brahman ka—vadh karne jakar kitna guruttar apradh kiya hai*" (4.13. p. 200). To him, Chanakya's wish is supreme: "*Aaj wahi hoga Gurudev, jo aagya hogi*" (4. 13. p. 201).[15]

Chandragupta obviously is a mortal; he is susceptible to joys and pains of life. Prasad's Chandragupta is torn within himself, his valour and chivalry notwithstanding. He expresses his inner struggle to Malvika:

> *Sangharsh Yuddh dekhna chaho to mera hridya pharkar dekho, Malvika. Asha aur nirasha ka yuddh, bhavon aur abhavon ka dwandva. Koi bhi nahin, phir bhi na jaane kaun meri sampoorn suchi mein riktachinh laga deta hai. Malvika, tum meri tambulvahini ho, mere vishwas ki, mitrata ki, pratikriti ho. Dekho, mein daridra hoon ki nahin, tumse mera koi rahasya gopniya nahin. Mere hridya main kuch hai ki nahin, tatolne se bhi nahin jan parta.* (4.4. p. 167)[16]

His involvement with Malvika was so much that her memory constantly pricks him in his pensive moods: he is absorbed by her thought: "*Pita gaye, mata gayee, Gurudev gaye, kandhe se kandha bhirakar pran dene wala chir sahchar Simharan gaya. To bhi Chandragupta ko rahna parega: parantoo Malvika, Ah! weh swargiya kusum!*" (4.4. p. 172). Roy's hold over Prasad is quite evident in the portrayal of Chandragupta.

In Prasad's play, Dandayan, a super human being, has been used to voice metaphysical values of ancient India's past. But, to set the record straight, the idea is not original; the playwright has taken it from Roy. Helen has referred to his father about one such philosopher, Diogenes (3.4. p. 76). Again, Simharan and Philips by Prasad are on the pattern of Roy's Chandraketu and Antigonus respectively.[17]

Chanakya has not only overshadowed Chandragupta and others on his side; he has been depicted too tall and towering to allow his opponents' emergence as compatible foil/antagonist. For example, Rakshas, Nand and Parvateshwar—all opponents of Chanakya are not more than straw men before Chanakya. In fact, Poru, the historical personage, has been run down by the playwright beyond redemption: he is killed by Kalyani when he is trying to seduce her. Similarly, Nand has also not attained the stature due to antagonists.

Rakshas, who is the key figure in *Mudrarakshas*, has been rendered as a hedonic person, mad after Suvasini, "*Jaata Magadh, kat ti praja, lut te nagar. Mein Suvasini ke liye Magadh bachana chahata tha.*" And when Suvasini says, "I am yours," he is overwhelmed, "*Suvasini. Kusumpur ka swargiya kusum. Main hastgat kar loon? Nahin, rajkop hoga. Parantoo jeevan vritha hai, meri vidya, mera parishkrit vichar sab vyarth hai. Suvasini ek laalsa hai, ek pyas hai. Weh amrit hai, use paane ke liye sau baar maroonga*" (1.4. pp. 60-61).

The women characters in the drama are Alka, Kalyani, Suvasini, Malvika and Cornelia. Of them, it is on Alka that Prasad has focussed his attention.[18] She comes into picture at the very start of the play and stays upto the last. She has been presented as a valiant fighter for the cause of national unity and independence. She revolts against his brother for his hobnobbing with the Greek. She is enamoured by Chanakya and Chandragupta and has developed attachment for Simharan for his patriotism. Both are comrades-in-arms. If Simharan thinks that "*Mera desh Malav hi nahin, Gandhar bhi hai. Yehi kya smagra Arya-vritta hai*" (1.1. p. 52), she also thinks that "*Main bhi Arya-vritta ki baalika hoon.*" Her love for Simharan and dedication for the country are inseparable. She rouses the masses to unitedly resist the Greek aggression: "*Himadri Tung, Shrung se/ Prabudh Shudh Bharti/Swayam Prabha Samujuwala/ Swatantrata Pukarti*" (4.6. p. 177).

Her finest hour comes when she finally prevails (4.6. p. 129) over her brother Ambhik to join the mainstream of freedom fighters, who assures her, "*Khadag ki shapath mein kartavya se chyut na hoonga.*"

Through Suvasini, Prasad has focused upon showing the plight of rather outcast women in the male-dominated social order. Suvasini turns to dancing in order to eke out her livelihood. In her childhood, she had an affair with Chanakya. When she joined Nand's drama party, Nand wanted to seduce her but she rebuffs him. She was rather attracted towards Rakshas and also wanted to marry him provided her father allowed.

Rakshas always suspected her infidelity with Chanakya which was far from the case, "*Thehro Amatya! main Chanakya ki idhar to ek prakar se vismrit ho hi gayee thi, tum soi huyee bhranti ko na jagao*" (4.2. p. 163). She never allows her chastity violated even by the powers that be.

In fact, she did not let Chanakya falter at one stage. Her dormant affection for Chanakya, however, did kindle after the incident and she was in two minds: whom to love, Rakshas or Chanakya. And when she opted for Chanakya, it was the latter who went to her rescue, rather repaid her debt, and did not allow her to falter. Her discourse with Cornelia about the fate of a married woman, in fact, shows an awakening and a desire to change the existing male-female dispensation.

Prasad has been very unkind to two women characters, Kalyani and Malvika, both in love with Chandragupta. Kalyani, the princess of Magadh, is imbued with deep love for Chandragupta, vindictiveness towards Parvateshwar and veneration for her father. Her love for Chandragupta was to such an extent that "*Kalyani ne varan kiya tha kewal ek purush ko, weh tha Chandragupta,*" but by the time Chandragupta came to know about it, it was too late, "*Parantoo tum mere pita ke virodhi huye. Ab mere liye kuch bhi avshisht na raha*" (4.1. p. 160). She commits suicide, paving the way for Chanakya's plan for Chandragupta's marriage with Cornelia. Prasad could have dispensed with her desperate act of ending her life.

Malvika's story is all the more pathetic. Acharya Nand Dulare Vajpayee[19] has written a full-fledged article on Malvika, praising Prasad's exquisiteness in featuring Malvika, as personification of women sacrifice in Indian tradition. Malvika, an accomplice of Alka, is imbued with patriotic and national feelings. She has never hesitated to work even under the most challenging circumstances for national cause. Simultaneously, she has developed intense love for Chandragupta, she adores him. He is her icon of love for whom no sacrifice on her part is too great. Chandragupta knows it. She is his confidante: "*Meri koi antrang nahin, tum bhi mujhe samraat kahkar pukarte ho*" (4.6. 167).

But what is in store for her at the hands of the playwright: she willingly and knowingly embraces death in order to save Chandragupta: "*Jaao priyatam, sukhi jeevan bitane ke liye, aur main rahti hoon chir dukhi jeevan ka ant karne ke liye*" (4.6 p. 169).

But the issue is, whether Prasad has not taken the idea of Malvika from Roy. Malvika's image is easily discerned in Chhayaa who has the same degree of pure and serene love for Chandragupta; "*Usi ka dhyan rahta hai*" (3.5. p. 77) or again "*Yadi mere ek hazaar jeevan hote to main anayaas hi subko unke charnon mein arpit kar deti. Dukh to isi baat ka hai ki unko dene ke liye mere paas kuch bhi nahin hai. Wahi hai ki unhe dene layak mere paas kuch nahin hai*" (4.6. p. 104).

And when she comes to know about compulsion of Chandragupta to marry Cornelia, she, like Malvika, gives her consent, too, willingly to Helen: "*Main swechha se apne hridya ki nidhi—apna sarvasva, tumko arpit karti hoon*" (5.1. p. 111) and when the memory of the past pricks, she consoles herself: "*Mere sarvasva . . . Chandragupta! . . . Nahin Chhaya, tum . . . nirmam hokar apni pravirti ka gala ghont do . . . main unke sukh mein hi sukhi rahoongi—Priyatam, tum sukhi raho, tumhara sukh hi mere jeevan ki saadhna bane*" (5.3. p. 121). Like Malvika, she bears her pain with fortitude: "*Sabhi vyathaon ko main bhogun, sab sukh ke bhagi tum ho, tum pranadhik sukhi raho, bus aur na kuch meri ichcha hai*" (5.3. p. 129). Compare it with Malvika's testament, "*O mere jeevan ki smriti! O antar ke aatur-anurag*" (4.4. p. 169).

Cornelia, Selucus's daughter, is drawn by Prasad on Helen's model. She is totally enamoured by Aryan culture and the playwright has used her to expound and extol ancient values of Indian culture. She is in deep love with Chandragupta, "*Mujhe Bharat ki seema se door ley chaliye, nahin to main paagal ho jaoongi.*" She is quite enlightened and disapproves her father's designs to attack India. Like Helen, she also reprimands Rakshas for betraying his country. She enters into wedlock with Chandragupta and considers it necessary for ushering in an era of lasting peace between the two great countries with rich cultural heritage. By all accounts, Prasad seems to have done very little to dress up Helen for making his Cornelia.

Art of Characterization

A scrutiny of both *Chandraguptas* bears out close affinity insofar as the craft of characterization is concerned. Both the playwrights have employed indirect and direct means to highlight personal traits/information of the characters.

Prasad provides information about Rakshas as being an accomplished artist in the very beginning of the play through citizens (1.2 p. 55). Roy, likewise, informs about Katyayan being the new minister (1.2). Similarly, it is through neighbours that one learns about Nand's hostility to Buddhists and to Chanakya's father (1.3 p. 58). The people also talk about the avaricious nature of Nand (1.3 p. 63).

About Chandragupta's innate qualities, one learns from Selucus, "*Yeh to koi bara sriman purush hai*" (1.10 p. 83), and Chanakya tells him, "*Yeh Chandragupta Magadh ka rajkumar hai*" (1.10. 83). It is through Alexander that one comes to know about Nand and his cruel nature (pp. 125,

127). Not merely that, Rakshas has been shown praising Chanakya: "*Chanakya, vilakshana budhi ka Brahman hai, uski prakhar pratibha kut rajniti ke saath din raat jaise khilwar kiya karti hai*" (3.1. p. 127). Parvateshwar does the same about Chandragupta, "*Chandragupta ke kshatriya hone ka pramaan. . . . Arya Chanakya, mein shamta rakhte huye jis kaam ko na kar saka weh karya nissahai Chandragupta ne kiya, Arya-vritta Yavnon ko nikal jaane ka sanket uske prachur bal ka dyotak hai. . . . Chandragupta Arya-vritta ka ekchhatra samraat hone ke upyukta hai*" (3.2 p. 129).

Roy's play is also replete with such circumstances. For instance, to Chandraketu's query to Chandragupta about Chanakya, Chandragupta tells him and the audience beforehand: "*Ati budhiman eknisht vichaksharn . . . vayu ke saath baatein karte hai . . . unki krudh drishti se jal jaate hain, bhasm ho jate hain, weh ekaaki rahte hain, jagat mein unka koi bandhu nahin hai*" (1.4. p. 21).

In both the plays, conflict is the prime mover of dramatic development and characterization. The conflict is both external and internal: the external being political, social, cultural, ethnic and religious. Apart from this, there is clash of personalities also.

The other aspect relates to the inner conflict of the characters themselves. Portrayal of the surge of feelings has been depicted through the devices of action, soliloquies and dialogues. The play is replete with soliloquies, long and short, in prose and verse. In Prasad's play there are 5 soliloquies ranging between 12-23 lines, of which 3 are by Chanakya, 1 each by Chandragupta and Parvateshwar, 24 soliloquies of the range between 4 to 10 lines. Of them, 4 by Alka, 3 each by Cornelia, Malvika, Rakshas and Chanakya, 2 by Chandragupta and Kalyani; 1 each by Nand,

Simharan, Gandhar Naresh and Dandayan. These soliloquies portray both external as well as inner conflict of the characters. In this respect, Prasad has followed Roy as the Bengali play is also characterized with monologues and soliloquies.

The device of dialogue has been effectively used to convey the plan of events and feelings of the characters by both the playwrights. The language is poetic and emotive, philosophical and passionate. For instance, Prasad in the very beginning of his play indicated the prevailing political scenario through the dialogue between Simharan and Chanakya.

Prasad has, however, used another piece of device—and this is his plus point over Roy—Malvika as a confidante of Chandragupta. Though a minor character, she is so near and dear to Chandragupta that in her presence, he opens his inner heart unreservedly.

Conclusion

All said and done, Prasad's characters leave an indelible impression of their individuality. They are human beings and suffer from human weaknesses. Even the tallest Chanakya is suffering from heartache. What is, however, disconcerting is, that he has not judiciously utilized his resources on diversifying his characterization.

Compared to the towering personality of Chanakya, everybody looks dwarfish—Chandragupta and the antagonists alike. Prasad has not created a counterfoil compatible to the stature of Chanakya. The things have come to such a pass that the issue as to who is the protagonist, Chanakya or Chandragupta, remains an open-ended question among the scholars.

The lopsidedness apart, he has unnecessarily run down the historic personage of Porus and resorted to Operation Kalyani-Malvika which he could have avoided.

Clearly, there is close affinity between the two plays in characterization. It is evident both in the use of dramatic devices and the overall pattern of characterization. A number of his characters, both major and minor, are found to follow the footsteps of their predecessors in Roy's play. They echo the same sentiments, show same state of mind, and react the same way in identical situations. The evidence suggests 'intertextuality.'

Yet in all fairness to Prasad, it may be said that in the final outcome, his characters bear the imprint of his own ideology, workmanship, sensibilities and imagination, Roy's hold notwithstanding. The message they convey is what Prasad has conceived for them.

NOTES

1. Nagendra, "Dramatic Art." *Jayshankar Prasad: His Mind and Art*, pp. 154-55.
2. Romila Thapar, "The Perennial Aryans," *Seminar*, p. 24.
3. This draws our attention to Roy's Chanakya who is equally sentimental: "*Katyayan . . . mein bara deen hoon. Chanakya kootnitgya, kaushal mein daksh aur vichhaksham hai. . . . Kintu mera hridya cheer kar dekho mitra. Yeh ek sooni marubhumi hai—isme karuna ka ek kan nahin hai, vishwas nahin hai*" (5.2. p. 122).

   And also mark another passage, "*Priti hinsa poorn ho gayee . . . baahar ke vaadya to tham gaye hain, parantoo ab hridya ka wahi hahakaar sunai par raha hai. Agaadh sneh rashi hridya mein hai, parantoo uske liye paatra koi bhi nahin hai. Kampit aagreh se man kisi ko chhati se lagana chahata hai, parantoo us vyagra aalingan mein chipat rahti hai kewal apni ushna nishwas.*" (4.1, p. 82)

4. This has a resonance of Roy's Chanakya when a girl with a beggar meets him, he is totally upset. "*Yeh kya? sahsa pranon mein krandan kyon ho utha? Yeh bhikshuk baalika hai. . . . Mere man mein durbalta kyon ayee*" (4.1). Mark the expression *durbalta*.
5. This apart, both the Chanakyas react in the same way after being humiliated by Nand. Prasad's Chanakya: "*Mein aaj pran karta hoon ki daya kisi se na maangoonga aur adhikar tatha avsar milne par kisi par na karoonga.*" Cf. Roy's, "*Mein kshama nahin, prithvi tal mein koi kisi ko kshama nahin karta, kar nahin sakta. . . . Sab kshama maukhik hai*" (3.6).
6. See Govind Chatak, *Prasad ke Natak: Swaroop Aur Sanrachna*, pp. 150-51; Bishambar Manav, *Prasad ke Paanch Natak*, pp. 55-56; Satyendra Taneja, *Hindi Natak: Punarmulyankan*, pp. 235-38.
7. "*Ishwar ne mera ghar shoonya karke meri stri ko—meri grahlakshmi ko--jabardasti chheen liya. . . . Daaku meri ladki ko har le gaye. . . . Kanya ke haran ne to meri reedh todh di hai . . . main kisi kaam se baahar gayaa tha, laut aakar dekha . . . kanya ki sej khaali hai. Tab meri dhamni me khoon ubal kar teji se daurne lagaa. Aankhon ke aage andhera chhaa gayaa. Dharti se ek garam bhaap aakaash ki or uthne lagi. Iske baad paagal ki tarah beti ko pukarta, chillaata hua, main raste mein daurne lagaa. Paas ke jungle mein jaakar khojta phira. Pakshi meri sahanubhuti mein kalah kar uthe. Nadi ke kinare jaakar kanya ko pukaarne laga. Us andhkar mein kewal nadi ke bahne ki dhwani ke aur koi na bola. Mein murchhit hokar gir para*" (1.2, pp. 16-18).
8. Cf. with Roy's: (i) "*Manushay ki is kritaghnata mein hi Chanakya ki rajniti ka janam hua hai. Mein manushay ki us kardam-kutsit pravartiyon ko kaam mein lagaata hoon*" (3.3. p. 64). He is not different from Prasad's. (ii) "*Podhe andhkar mein badhte hain aur meri niti lata bhi usi bhanti vipatti tam mein lehlahati hogi. Haan, kewal shaurya se kaam nahin*

chalega. Ek baat samajh lo. Chanakya sidhi dekhta hai, saadhan chahe kaise hi haun" (2.2. p. 97).

9. Dasrath Ojha, *Hindi Natak: Udbhav aur Vikas*, p. 359.
10. Perhaps Ojha noted that Roy's Chanakya rather stops Chandragupta from killing him using the same metaphor: *Chanakya (haath uthakar, chillakar) kehta hai: "Vadh mat karo! bandi banao.*" (2.5. p. 54).
11. Roy's Chanakya has the same vision: "*Brahman ka pratap abhi mita nahin. . . . Ishwar moorkh nahin hai jo usne shareer mein mastishk ko bujaoon ke upar banaya hai. Arya rishijan moorkh nahin thei. . . . Bharat jab tak Bharat hai tab tak yeh Brahman hi samaj ka shaasan karega*" (3.6. p. 83).
12. Maheshwar, *Hindi Bangla Natak*, pp. 176-77; Birendra Narayan, *Hindi Drama and Stage*, p. 183; Sudhakar Chattopadhyaya, *Adhunik Hindi Sahitye Banglaar Sthan*, p. 57.
13. Birendra Narayan, p. 183.
14. Roy's Chandragupta felt the same way and reacted the same way when he was informed about Chanakya's decision to execute Nand: "*Brahman ki itni spradha ho gayee ki mujhe samachar tak nahin diya—mujhse anumati nahin maangi. Ascharya! . . . jaise main is saamrajya mein kuch bhi nahin hoon—Chanakya ke haath ka yantramatra hoon*" (3.5. p. 73).

    He again shows his resentment in the same vein over the cancellation of victory festival by Chanakya: "*Mujhe lagta hain ki main apne saamrajya mein hi bandi hoon, apne ghar mein naukar hoon. . . . yadi hum dono ke beech main yahi sambandh hai to yeh bandhan jitna shighra chhinn ho sake utna hi achcha hai*" (4.2 p. 89). And when Chanakya behaves in Prasad's way, Chandragupta reacts the same way: "*Jahan Chanakya nahin hai, wahan kya raajkaaj nahin chalta. Itna ahankar! Bura kya hai. Aaj main mukta hoon—swatantra hoon. Aaj main sachmuch maharaj hoon*" (4.2. p. 91).

15. Roy's Chandragputa expresses his gratitude similarly: "*Meri is keerti ke Vidhata Gurudev hi hain. Yeh sab aap hi ke charnon ki kripa hai*" (5.5. p. 137).
16. Roy's Chandragupta was also susceptible to human feelings which are evident from his dilemma to combat Nand, his brother: "*Uske upar chalane ke liye talwar uthate hi mere pita ka rakta hridya ke pind mein uchal para aur pasliyon mein jor se takkar markar chilla utha--'khabardar Chandragupta, yeh tera bhai hai—Magadha ka saamrajya kya bhai se bara hai*'" (2.5. p. 59).
17. Satyendra Taneja, pp. 241-44. Bishambar Manav, pp. 48-49. Parmeshwari Lal Gupta, *Prasad ke Natak*, p. 96.
18. Parmeshwari Lal Gupta, pp. 11-12. Jaganath Sharma, *Prasad ke Natakon ka Shastriya Adhyayan*, p. 165.
19. "*Malvika: Ek Sanketik Parit*," *Jayshankar Prasad*, pp. 115-21.

Language and Diction

Critics[1] have noted similarity in 'language and expression between the two texts,' particularly in the use of ornate, abstrusive and a Sanskritized language punctuated with lyricism, symbology, metaphors, images, personification, allegory and so on. A critic has described D.L Roy's language as "*Uchhvaasit hridyaveg mandit tatha alankar bahul*"[2] which, except Rabindranath Tagore, has no precedence in Bengali literature. Ramchandra Shukla has noted influence of Bengali on Prasad: "*Sanskrit ki komalkant padavali se yukta bangbhasa ke sahityanushilan ne padlalitye ko jo goonj Prasad ji ke man me samai weh baraabar bani rahi.*"[3]

Process of Sanskritization

While the Sanskritized form of language has a historical context, much of its emotiveness and lyricism can be attributed to their romantic background. The process of Sanskritization and development of 'chaste' literary Bengali (and later Hindi) started in the colonial period. Macaulay's minute and Bentick's 1835 resolution in favour of English only sounded the death-knell of indigenous Sanskrit learning. The spread of English education roused the minds of *bhadraloks* for creating an exclusive language of culture for their own use. The problem was resolved by developing a Bengali language and literature which had the sophistication of Sanskrit and secularity of English to suit the growing new social class. A literary Bengali called

Sadhubhasha developed in the process as the lingo of *Bhadraloks*. It was a Sanskritized Bengali language. Sanskritization also helped them to forge alliances with the elite members of the other Indian linguistic groups who were also going through the same process of moulding their respective languages in a similar direction.

The Arya Samaj played an important role towards the development of a lingua franca of the reformed Hindus or the 'Aryas,' Hindi soon acquired the title of 'Aryabhasha' (the language of the Aryas) and its Sanskritized form became part of the movement's vision of a reformed Hindu society. Arya Samaj leaders took an active part in the campaign for the popularization of the Devnagri script (as distinct from the prevalent script of Urdu) and its acceptance for official use. The Nagari Pracharini Sabha was set up in Benares in the final years of the nineteenth century. The Hindi-Urdu differentiation had come to the fore. Mahavir Prasad Dwivedi, the father of Hindi prose, undertook the Cleansing Operation and Sanskritized *Khariboli* was chosen and the Urdu heritage was deodorized. It was this Sanskritized *Khariboli* in which *Chhayavaad* injected lyricism. The result was, to quote Jayshankar Prasad, "*Shabd vinyas mein aisa paani chara ki usme ek tarap utpan karke sookshm abhivyakti ka pryas kiya gaya.*"[4]

Language

The language used in *Chandragupta* is essentially Chhayavadi prose, '*Pheelpaanvi*,' to quote Nalin Vilochan Sharma, a noted Hindi scholar.[5] Here are few examples: "*ek agnimey gandhak ka strot Arya-vratta ke loh-astragaar me ghuskar visfot karega. Chanchala ran-lakshmi indradhanush si vijai-maala haath me liye us sunder neel-lohit pralya-jalad me vichran karegi aur veer kridya mayur se naachenge*" (1.1. p. 51); "*Han, Han rahasya hai. Yavan-aakraman kariyo ke pushkal-swaran se pulkit hokar Arya-vratta ki sukh-rajni ki shanti-nidra mein utrapath ko argala dhire se khol dene ka rahasya hai*" (1.1. p. 49); "*Main Brahman hoon. Mera samrajya karuna ka tha. Mera dharm prem ka tha. Anand-Samudra mein shanti deep . . . anant aakaash vitan tha, Shasyashaamal kamal vishwambhara meri shayia thi*" (4.4 p. 171).

However, in the emotive moments, the language becomes all the more ornate: "*Phool hanste huye aate hain. phir makrand girakar murjha jaate hain, aansu se dharti ko bhigokar chale jaate hain! Ek snigdha sameer ka jhonka aata hai, nishvaas phenk kar chalaa jaata hai. Kya prith-vital rone ke liye hi hai?*" (2.4 p. 104); "*Akasmaat jeevan-kaanan main, ek raaka-rajni ki chhayaa mein chhipkar madhur vasant ghus aata hai. Shareer ki sab kyariyan hari bhari ho jaati hain. Saundraya ka kokil 'Kaun'? kehkar sabko rokne tokne lagta hai, pukarne lagta hai. Rajkumari! Phir usi main prem ka mukul lag jaata hai, aansu-bhari smrityan makrand-si unmein chhipi rahti hain*" (4.9 p. 188).

The use of 'chaste' and ornate language in the Hindi play has often been made to portray inner conflict, spiritual aspect of Indian culture, nature and landscape. The same pattern is observed in the Bengali drama.

A characteristic of the language of Prasad's drama relates to the impact of Shaivite philosophy of *Prityobhijya darshan* and *anandvad* on him. For example, use of such words as '*bhuma*,' '*aanand,*' '*madhu,*' '*samras,*' '*pralaya.*' In the same way, the Bengali play chooses words and language appropriate to address Mother Goddess who is worshipped in Bengal; Chanakya's monologue, "*Shukar ka mukh*" (2.2. pp. 35-36) already quoted, and use of expressions like *Meri Prayesi, Hai Adrashya, Mahashakti, Maheshwari, Patitpavni, Mata Vasundhara* are some examples.

Prasad's play has employed words which were frequently used in the freedom struggle, such as *Swadhinta, Swatantrata, Paradhinta, daasta, vidroh, utpiran. nirih janta. rashtra, desh-drohi, kuchakra*. Such words are not used in the Bengali drama. Rather it has used a different set of words reflecting socio-economic condition such as *durbhiksha, kankal, bhookh ki jwala*.

The language is, however, not abstruse everywhere; it depends upon the situation: "*Chanakya: Chhokriyon se baat karne ka samay nahin hai, Maurya*!" (2.4 p. 105).[7]

Diction

Prasad's drama is interspersed with long speeches particularly to express either inner conflict or patriotic feelings. Take for instance, Chanakya's soliloquy when he is lodged in Magadh jail: "*Sameer ki gati bhi avarudh hai. . . . mein pralay ke samaan abadhgati aur kartavya mein Indra ke vajra ke samaan bhayanak banoonga*" (1.7. pp.72-73); or "*Chanakya: Utrapath ke pramukh gantantra. . . . Chandragupta ko hi un logon ne bhi senapati banaaya hai*" (2.6. pp.113-14). Again, Alka's patriotic exhortation: "*Bhai! Ab bhi tumhara bhram nahin gayaa. Rajya kisi ka nahin hai. . . . Ujjwal aalok se mandit hokar Gandhar rajkul amar ho jayegaa*" (4.6. pp.178-79).[8]

It is in the frequent use of some common symbols and imagery that a close similarity between the two plays is revealed. These are: '*Samundra*,' '*nadi*,' '*aakash*,' '*megh*,' '*agni*,' '*daavanal*,' '*godhuli*, '*bijli*,' '*Indradhanush*,' '*Chandra*,' '*dhumraashi*,' '*Indra*,' '*kanak rashmiyan*,' '*van*,' '*pushp*,' '*makrand*,' '*madhu*' (it is Prasad's favourite); '*Himadri*,' '*giri*,' '*shikhar*,' '*shrang*' etc.

The Bangla *Chandragupta* provides examples of '*laakshrinkta*' (allegory): "*Chandragupta: Suna hai ki ve vayu ke saath baat karte hain. Agni ke saath mantrana karte hain. Unki krudh drishti se tan jal uthte hain . . . bhasm ho jaate hain. Ve ekaaki rahte hain, jagat me unka koi bhi bandhu nahin hai*" (1.4. p. 21); "*Eendhan prastut karo, Chandragupta! Main us se brahm tej prajwalit karoonga. Weh agni davaanal ke samaan vyapt ho jayegee. Samast Bharatvarsh dhadhak uthega. . . . Chandragupta*" (1.4. p. 26); "*Jeebh ko laplapaate huye bhookhe kutton ko yudhkshetra mein chhor diya hai. Ab ve swachhand bhaav se bhishn rakt dhaara ki paan karte rahen is nivirvan me vyaghr aur bhaalooyon ki kami ko aaj ye kutte poora kare . . . vyaghr aur bhaaloo peit bharne ka anya upaai na hone ke kaaran manushya ke rakt ka paan karte hain; aur manushya, lobh ke kaaran, vicharheen hinsa mein lipt hokar, ek doosre ki gardan mein daant gaadate hain*" (2.5. p. 47).

Probably, taking a clue from Roy's "*Eendhan prastut karo*," Prasad has developed the idea in an artistic manner in his "*Ek agnimay gandhak ka strot*" (1.1. p. 49). Similarly, Roy's "*Jeebh ko laplapaate . . . daant gaarte hain*" is fashioned in the Hindi play as "*Simharan: Maanav kab daanav se bhi durdaant, pashoo se bhi barbar aur pathar se bhi kathor karuna ke liye niravkaash hridyawaala ho jayega, nahin kaha ja sakta*" (1.1. p. 52). Mark that the sense in both the passages is the same.

Likewise, "*Helen: Surya ast ho gaya. Is drishya ko dekhkar aaj sindhu tat ka weh garimamaya suryaast yaad aa rahaa hai*" (2.1. p. 30) has been used by Prasad as

"*Chanakya: Kitna gauravmaya aaj ka arunodaya hai*" (4.13. p. 199).

The use of metaphors is found in plenty in both the plays: "*Helen: Hinsa apne sahastra phanon ko phelakar dauri aa rahi hai aur yeh sansaar mugdh drishti se uski aur dekh rahaa hai*" (4.3. p. 95). Here 'hinsa' (violence) has been compared to serpent. Again, take another example: "*Antigonus: Us maansik vyadhi ki marm-pira ko, jiske vyang se vikshipt hokar main aakaash se toot-te huye taare ke samaan prithvi par chakkar kaat-ta phirta hoon. Singh ki garjan, Vyaghra ki jhapat, agni ki lapat, bijli ki karak aur shatru ke khadag ki avahelana karke main us vyang ki vedna se vyakul hokar aandhi prithvi ka chakkar kaat-ta huya tumhaare paas aayaa hoon*" (4.4. p. 96). Examples from Prasad may be seen in the passages quoted in the sequel.

There are examples in both the plays of using abstract for concrete: "*Hinsa apne samast phano ko phelakar dauri aa rahi hai*" (Roy's *Chandragupta*); in Prasad, "*Ek agnimay gandhak ka strot*" (already cited); "*Arya-vratta ka bhavishya likhne ke liye koochakra aur pratarna ki lekhni aur masi prastut ho rahi hai*" (1.1. p. 47).

There are examples of personification: for example, "*Phool hanste huye aate hain*" (Prasad's *Chandragupta*, already cited); and in Roy, the opening passage of the play, "*Sachmuch Selucus! Yeh kaisa vichitra desh hai . . .*" (already cited).

Both the plays are interspersed with poems and songs, lyrical prose apart. In the course of reading Prasad's *Chandragupta*, one encounters imprint of Roy's play. Here are some examples:

(i) "*Cornelia: Pitaji, yeh paap ki malin chhayaa hai. Uski bhavon me kitna andhkaar hai, aap dekhte na-*

hin. Us se alag rahiye. Vishram kijiye. Vijayon ki pravanchna mein apne ko na hariye. Mahatvakaanksha ke daav par manusheyata sadev haari hai"; (4.7. p. 184); "*Helen: Pitaji, is vishwa-pariwaar ko videsh aur ahemkaar ne jis prakaar ek doosre se prathak kar diya hai, usi prakar se nadi-parvaton ne nahin kiya*" (Roy's *Chandragupta*, 4.3. p. 95)

(ii) "*Chanakya: Kya? Meri durbalta? Nahi*" (4.3. p. 165). And in Roy: "*Chanakya: Yeh kya? Sehsa praanon me krandan kyon ho utha? Yeh bhikshuk baalika hai . . . mere man me durbalta kyon aayee*?" (4.1. p. 85).

(iii) "*Philips: Nahin, kumari Saamragyi kaho*" (2.1. p. 90); "*Helen: Helen nahin, rajkumari*" (Roy's 2.1. p. 29).

(iv) "*Chandragupta: Sangharsh! Yudh dekhna chaho to mera hridya phaar kar dekho, Malvika*" (Prasad's *Chandragupta*, 4.4. p. 167); "*Chanakya: Parantoo mere hridya ko chirkar bheetar dekho*" (Roy's *Chandragupta*, 5.2. p. 115); "*Chanakya: Yeh vaksha (sehsa Chandragupta ka haath pakarkar apne vaksha par rakhta hai) . . . is vaksha par haath rakh kar dekho!. . . kya dekhte ho*" (Roy's *Chandragupta*, 1.4. p. 25).

(v) "*Raja: Boorha ho chala parantoo man boorha nahin huya. Bahut dinon tak trishna ko tript karta raha, par tripti nahin hoti*" (Prasad's *Chandragupta*, 1.8. p. 75); "*Helen: Kirti nahin, apkirti . . . purush ki aakaanksha vichitra hai. Weh kabhi poori nahin hoti*!" (Roy's *Chandragupta*, 2.1. p. 27).

(vi) "*Chanakya: Katyayan ab kewal Panini se kaam nahin chalega. Arthshastra aur dand-niti ki aavashykata hai*" (Prasad's *Chandragupta*, 1.7. p. 73); "*Isi se matiameit ho gaya . . . rehne do. Mere paas Panini ke liye samay nahin hai. . . . Vyakaran se kaam nahin chalega*" (Roy's *Chandragupta*, 2.1. p. 37)

(vii) "*Simharan: Malav kabhi bandi nahi ho sakta*" (1.1. p. 49) and "*Chandragupta: Usey koi bandi nahin bana sakta hai*" (Prasad's *Chandragupta*. 1.1. p. 49). And in Roy's play, "*Chandragupta: Vadh kiye bina mujhe koi bandi nahin bana sakta*" (1.1. p. 7).

(viii) "*Sikandar: Yeh adbhut desh hai*" (2.1. p. 92); "*Sikandar: Sachmuch Selucus! yeh kaisa vichitra desh hai*" (Roy's *Chandragupta*, 1.1. p. 3).

(ix) "*Chandragupta: adhik harsh, adhik unnati ke baad hi to adhik dukh aur patan ki baari aati hai*" (Prasad's *Chandragupta*, 4.5. p. 172); "*Katyayan: Sukh aur dukh manushya ke jeevan ke saath jure huye hain. Aalok aur andhkaar ke beech me se hokar samay aage barh jaata hai*" (Roy's *Chandragupta*, 1.2. p. 12).

(x) "*Malvika: Jaao Priytam! sukhi jeevan bitane ke liye, aur main rehti hoon chir dukhi jeevan ka ant karne ke liye*" (Prasad's *Chandragupta*, 4.4. p. 169); "*Chhayaa: Main vyatha se grasit priyatam! Tum karo sukh bhog nitnav. Tum hanso, hanste raho priye, Main virah jarjit priyatam*" (Roy's *Chandragupta*, 5.3. p. 122).

(xi) "*Chandragupta: Gurudev, vishwas rakhiye. . . . yeh Chandragupta aapke charnon ki shapathpurvak pratigya karta hai ki Yavan yahan kuchh na kar sakenge*" (Prasad's *Chandragupta*. 1.1. p. 51); "*Chanakya: Bahut achcha (Chandragupta ke prati) to tum mere per chhookar shapath lo ki is Brahman ke aadesh ka tum sarvatha paalan karoge*" (Roy's *Chandragupta*, 1.4. p. 25)

Conclusion

There is a clear impact of the Bengali play on Prasad's *Chandragupta.* But that does not imply 'imitation.' Prasad's play has a distinct individuality and its language has its own charm. It is Prasad's own creativity, his Chhayawadi background and Anandwadi philosophy that have provided a distinct flavour to the play.

NOTES

1. Maheshwar, *Hindi Bangla Natak*, p. 200. Govind Chatak, *Prasad ke Natak: Swaroop Aur Saranchana*, p. 234; K.C. Tyagi, "*Dwijendra Lal Roy Aur Prasad ke Natakon ka Tulnatamak Adhyayan.*"
2. Sudhakar Chattopadhyaya, *Adhunik Hindi Sahitye Banglaar Sthan*, p. 64.
3. Acharya Ram Chandar Shukla, *Hindi Sahitya ka Itihas*, p. 647.
4. Jayshankar Prasad, *Kavya aur kala tatha anye nibandh,* p. 112.
5. Cited Namvar Singh, "*Bhasha-Shaili,*" Indranath Madan, ed., *Prasad Pratibha*, p. 241.
6. The Bengali play has the same characteristics. Take for instance the opening passage of the play: "*Sikander: Sachmuch Selucus! Yeh kaisa vichitra desh hai. Din mein prachand surya iske neel aakash ko tapa deta hai aur raatri mein aakar shubhra chandra us aakash ko jyotsna se snaan kara jaata hai. Andhkarbhari raatri ke asankhya ujjwal nakshatra jab iske aakaash ko aalokit karte hain, tab main vismai aur aatank se us drishya ko dekhta reh jaata hoon. Varsha ritu mein prakaand detya-sena ke samaan guru gambheer garjan karti huyee shyamal megh mala jab aakash ko aachhadit kar deti hai tab main awaak hokar us drishya ko dekhta rehta hoon. Is desh mein tusharaveshtit himadri apne shrangon se gagan ko bhedta huya sthir bhaav se shaant*

khara huya hai. Iske vishaal nad-nadi uddam veg se pheni uchhvaas bikherte ja rahe hain. Iska marusthal tapt baaluka-rashi ke saath svechhachari ke samaan nirantar krira karta rehta hain" (1.4, p. 3); "*Chhayaa: Ye maano Devraj Indra ke saakshat avtaar hain. Inka darshan maano poorn chandra ka udai hai. Inka swar mano ranvaadhya hai. Jis samay in-hone dada ka aalingan kiya us samay aisa lagaa maano suryarashmi ne shaardiya megh ko achhadit kar liya ho*" (1.4, p. 22); "*Chanakya: Shukar ka mukh, makri ki khaal, shavdah ki gandh, arand ka swaad, aur gandarbh ka swar—in sabko milakar karai mein charha diya gaya hai. Dekhta hoon ki in sabke mishran se kaun sa padarth banta hai. Nis-chaya hi koi vyanjan taiaar hoga. . . . Hei adrashya maha-shakti! kitne durgandmaye gaddhe mein tum mujhko haath pakarkar le jaa rahi ho. Tumhari balihaari! (baahar jhank kar) Oh! baahar aus ki boonde maano jal rahi hain . . . jaise aag ki chingaariyan ho. Saara aakash jhulas jhulas kar dig-dha utpann kar raha hai . . . aur maine, is agnidah me apne ko jhonk diya hai. Main swyam bhasm nahin ho rahaa hoon . . . kewal apne brahmtej ke kaaran (attahaas karta hai) Na-hin, is kalyug me bhi sabko Brahman ka prataap dikhana hoga . . . hai, na pryesi tum apne lambe daant dikhakar at-tahas kar rahi ho. Apna jatajoot hila kar swikriti de rahi ho! . . . tum kitni kutsit ho . . . kitni sundar ho!! . . . tumhare prem mein kahin main paagal na ho jaaoon! (ekdam chaunk kar) kaun Katyayan*" (2.2, pp. 35-36).

7. And compare it with Roy's and mark the echo: "*Chanakya: Is samay naari ki vinti sunne ka samay nahin hai*" (2.2. p. 34).
8. Roy's drama exhibits the same characteristics. Take for instance, Antigonus's monologue in first scene of Act three: "*Yeh log apne ghar laut rahe hai . . . chirkaal tak sambhaav se kallol karte raho*" (pp. 56-57). It has 44 lines. Again: "*Chanakya tum nahin jaante yeh wahi tumhari maata hai janni hai*" (2.5. pp. 51-52).

The Difference in the Texts: Ideology

It needs no reiteration that there is subtle but very organic link between a writer's world-view and his work. The writer's individual vision is forged in the smithy of forces that impinge upon life. This piece attempts to examine the difference in the texts' ideology.

The question of a dramatic text's point of view and of its socio-political evaluation of reality is always a problematic one, for, in the system of discourses that constitutes the text, there is no authorial presence (even if there is an authorial discourse) and yet the ideology of the author cannot but be present in the way the diverse voices are perceived in their inter-relationship: It is either in the dialogic tension arising out of the opposition between different accents or in the moments of the inner conflicts of the characters that we may sense the presence of the authorial intention. It is also necessary to remember, as Pierre Vilar thought fit to remind his readers in his celebrated essay on 'Don Quixote,' that masterpieces have a date too.[1] These plays, which delve into India's ancient past, were published in the colonial era. The Bengali play *Chandragupta* in 1911 (i.e. in the hectic days of Swadeshi movement) and Hindi *Chandragupta* in 1931 when Gandhian nationalism had captured the imagination of the masses and anti-imperialist struggle had intensified. An analysis of how the plays interpret the social and ideological world of their times through the medium of the past would serve to illuminate our understanding, inter alia, of 'colonial consciousness.'

Perspectives of the Playwrights

Jayshankar Prasad's and D.L. Roy's fascination for India's past was in line with the temper of their era. Their purpose in turning to the past was to awaken a dormant, sullen and broken people to discover its glorious heritage.

For, the endeavour of a subjected people to reclaim the uninterrupted development of their history cannot but be based on the strength of their tradition. Therefore, an emphasis on the past, "a return to the sources," as Amil Cabral called it.[2] 'National liberation' is necessarily a cultural act.[3] Thus, in response to the colonial cultural hegemonization, there was an attempt to assert the identity of indigenous cultural tradition.

Prior to writing *Chandragupta* Prasad made sure of the facts from authentic sources. In *Vishakh* (1921), he expressed his ideas about his recourse to history in these words:

> The medium of history is vitally important for a people to discover for itself its own eternal values. For, it is quite sceptical that apart from looking back to our past civilization, as our guide, there is any other way which is more appropriate to our milieu for redeeming our self-esteem. What I cherish is that I ought to highlight such episodes from the unilluminating regions of India's history that account for the present state of things.[4]

D.L. Roy who chose the ancient India for the first time, explained his purpose of writing *Chandragupta* in these words:

> While Muslim historians have concealed their defeats, they have, left adequate material for writing the play. The Hindu historians, on the other hand, have even put a lid on their saga of victories. Rather, they have been too preoccupied

> with thoughts of *Varna* distinctions. The discriminations in the *Varna* system constitute the base of the present drama.[5]

However, any view of history depends as much on the eye of the beholder as on the source material.[6] Hence the gross bias in history writing is to be seen.[7]

The Ideological Ambience of Late 19th and Early 20th Century

Association of ideology with the interpretation of early Indian history goes back to the very beginning of modern historical investigation into India's past.[8] In the colonial era, the history of India was written with three perspectives: the Orientalists or Indologists; the British Utilitarianists and the Nationalist historians. The Indologists made the study of Sanskrit language and literature as *sine qua non* for reconstruction of India's past. They planted several myths in the Indian mind. One of them was the belief that Aryans and Dravidians were intact races, which has been rejected now as baseless and incorrect. Another myth was the notion of a 'golden age' of India resplendent in her pristine and spiritual glory. Indeed, the appeal of such a notion remains undiluted to this day. All ancient civilizations have rather entertained the ideas of superiority, be it Greeks or Romans or Chinese.[9] A colonized people needed that myth as one of the "sources of the self."[10]

The English Utilitarian ideologue, James Mill, propounded that Indians were incapable of self-government and they had been accustomed to despotic rule throughout. This was the Theory of Oriental Despotism. The viewpoint of the 'nationalist school' can be summed up in the words of J.D.M. Derrett: "The *dharmashastra* had been projected by patriots as proof that Indians were quite capable of organizing their own affairs justly and efficiently before the foreigners came, and without 'Oriental despotism.' The implication was that they were . . . inherently capable of sharing in their own government, and even monopolizing it as to rendering European superfluous."[11] The 'nationalists' upheld the myths propagated by the Indologists.[12]

Indian nationalism was conceived as an all-India ideology to fight against colonialism-imperialism and that India existed as a nation even in the ancient times—another myth because nation is a modern concept, something that arose in the course of the anti-colonial movement itself. Antonio Gramsci has commented on such a historical myth of the 'nation' in these words:

> the rhetorical prejudice (originating in literature according to which the Italian nation has always existed, from ancient Rome to the present day. This and other totems and intellectual conceits, although politically useful in the period of national struggle as a means of stirring up and concentrating energies, are critically inept and become, ultimately, a weakness."[13]

Tod's romantic myth-making about Rajput chivalry filled the nostalgic feelings of the golden past—a Hindu past—and it in turn, gave birth to what Bipan Chandra calls, "vicarious nationalism." The Muslims also began to develop their own variety of "vicarious nationalism."

Patriotism was seen as a part of religion. Both Aurobindo and Bipanchandra Pal identified patriotism with religion culminating into the symbol of Mother. Ranade and Lajpat Rai also underlined the spiritual aspects of nationalism and Annie Besant declared that 'patriotism and religion must join hands in India.' Vivekanand also made patriotism an integral part of religion.[14] The Swadeshi mood in general was closely associated with attempts to combine politics with religious revivalism.[15]

In the nineteenth century and, of course, well into the twentieth century, the text of *Bhagavad Gita* acquires a 'status of 'the Book' as the term is normally understood in the Semitic religion. A number of nationalists like Tilak, Sri Aurobindo, Vivekanand and Gandhi wrote commentaries on *Gita.*

The cultural-ideological struggle in colonial India upto 1920s assumed two dimensions. The first, a struggle against the backward elements of traditional culture and the second, against the hegemonizing influences of colonial culture.

The struggle against traditional culture embraced a variety of issues concerning caste and religion, marriage and family, education and language and so on. The opposition to caste was total and uncompromising in ideas, if not always in practice. It was looked upon as morally and ethically abhorrent, socially debilitating and politically divisive. Even Dayanand supported *Chaturvarna* on the basis of virtue. Gandhi repeatedly harped on the evils of untouchability. The volunteers of Non-cooperation campaign were asked to sign a pledge for removing untouchability from their personal life.

On the political plane, with the emergence of Gandhi, a new era of mass mobilisation ushered in 1920s—witnessed Non-cooperation upsurge, revolutionary terrorism and the call to Purna Swaraj.

The nineteenth century socio-religious reform movement devoted considerable attention to the improvement of the position of women. Consequently, Sati was forbidden (1828), widow remarriage legalized (1856), and with Age of Consent Act (1891), marriage of a girl below twelve years of age was prohibited. Alongside, the movement for female education started, with the Christian missionaries and the Brahmos leading and the enlightened Hindus cooperating. Twentieth century saw the emergence of mass national movements, with women's participation in the public sphere. The ideology of nationalism proved a potent force for women to organize and protest, to lead demonstrations and go to jail. Participation in the freedom struggle was not a prerogative of the upper few. Western women like Margaret Cousins and Annie Besant, inspired their counterparts to build organizational networks such as the All India Women's Conference, 1927. The Child Marriage Restraint Act of 1929, which fixed the minimum age of marriage for a boy at eighteen and for a girl at fifteen, made it possible for them to realize their ambition.

World-View of the Plays

The world-view of both the dramas is very much influenced by 'Orientalist' and 'nationalist' discourse, albeit, there is marked divergence of perceptions and thrust. The theory of Aryan race and the uniqueness of Indian culture, are the running refrains of both the dramas.

While Cornelia is immersed in Aryan culture from head to toe: "*Yeh yavan bala sir se per tak Arya Sanskriti mein pagi hai*" (Prasad's *Chandragupta*, 4.6 p. 174); Helen wants to learn Sanskrit, "*Main Sanskrit bhasha seekhoongi sunte hain Sanskrit bhasha mein bhavukata, kavitavya aur gyan ka apoorva bhandaar hai*" (Roy's *Chandragupta*, 21. p. 30). This testifies to the influence of indologists.

The occidental thesis about India has also been debunked in both the plays. "*Anessacretes: Mujhe to yeh log aalsi maloom parte hain./Alexander: Nahin Nahin . . . yeh adbhut desh hai*" (Prasad's *Chandragupta* 2.1, p. 92). And in Roy's play, the same metaphor is used by Alexander (1.1, p. 3).

The fulsome praise by the Greek—Alexander and Cornelia/Helen—of India's cultural heritage is the world-view of the early nationalists. For example: "*Helen: Bharat ne Arya yug mein samast Asia ko aalokit kiya tha*" (Roy's *Chandragupta*, 4.3 p. 95) and to Cornelia, India is "*Swapnon ka desh, yeh tyag aur gyan ka paalna, yeh prem ki rangbhoomi. Anya desh manushyon ki janambhoomi hai; yeh bharat maanavta ki janambhoomi hai*" (Prasad's *Chandragupta*, 3.2 p. 131).[16]

Varna Ideology and the Vision of Brahman India

Varna ideology is the hallmark of both the plays but there is a difference in its presentation. The *Varna* hierarchy is *sui generis* of the social structure of Hindus which, to quote *Manu Smriti*: "For the sake of the preservation of this entire creation (*Purusha*) the exceedingly resplendent one, assigned separate duties to the classes which has sprung from his mouth, arms, thighs and feet. Teaching, studying, performing sacrificial rites, so too making others perform sacrificial rites, study and non-attachment to sensual pleasures—these be assigned to the Brahmans. Protection of the people, giving way of wealth, performance of sacrificial rites, study and non-attachment to sensual pleasures—these are in short, the duties of *Kshatriya*. Tending of cattle, giving way of wealth, performance of sacrificial rites, study, trade and commerce, usury and agricultural—these are the occupation of a *Vaishya*. The Lord has prescribed only one occupation (*karma*) for the Shudra, namely service without malice of . . . these other three classes."[17]

This ideology is articulated in *Chandragupta* in these words: "*Brahmatva ek sarvbhom shashvat budhi vaibhav hai. Weh apni raksha ke liye itne vanon ka sangthan kar lega*" (Prasad's *Chandragupta*, 1.10 p. 80). And furthermore, "*Chanakya: Tere poshak Vaishya, sewak shudra aur rakshak kshatriya hain*" (Prasad's *Chandragupta*, 1.9, p. 81).

The Bengali play has expressed more or less similar views: "*Brahmatva ke prataap ka kabhi lop nahin hota. Ishwar moorkh nahin hai jo usne shareer me mastishk ko bhujaon ke upar banaya hai. Arya rishi jan moorkh nahin the jinke anusaar Brahman Kshatriya se upar hai.*" (3.6 p. 75). The hegemony of *brahmanvad* and vision of a Brahman India has been propounded in both the plays: "*Rashtra ka Shubhchintan kewal Brahman hi kar sakta hai*" (Prasad's *Chandragupta*). According to the Bengali play, "*Yeh gaur varna jaati aaj bhi swaran sootra ke samaan samast samaaj ko goonthe huye hai*" (1.2 p. 11); "*Jisko koi bhi nahin kar sakta usko Brahman kar deta hai. Yeh Bharat desh jab tak Bharat hai tab tak samaj mein Brahman shasan karega*" (3.6. p. 76). The vision of a Brahman India is evident from the following: "*Katyayan: (to Chanakya) Brahman ke usi lupt tej ka aao hum dono milkar punarudhar kare. . . Jab tak Bharat Bharat bana huya hai, tab tak Brahman Brahman bana rahega*" (1.2. p. 13) Though it views the origin of *Varnas* stemming from supernatural sanction and in line with *Manu Smriti* declares: "*Brahman na kisi ke rajya mein rehta hai aur na kisi ke ann se palta hai. Swaraj mein vicharta hai aur amrit hokar jeeta hai.*" This is exactly the same as is laid down in *Manu Smriti*.[18]

> *swayemev brahmane bhudakte swam vaste swa*
> *dadati cha, aa nrishansyad brahmanasya bhunje dwitare jagaa* (101)

The drama has also attempted to elaborate the quintessence of devout Brahman at a number of places: "*Main Brahman hoon. Mera Samrajya karuna ka tha. Mera dharm prem ka tha. Anand-samundra mein shaanti dweep ke avishwasi Brahman main, chander-surya-nakshatra mere deep the, anant aakash vitaan tha, shasya shyamal komal vishambhara meri shayaa thi. Boddhik vinod karam tha, santosh dhan tha*" (4.4 p. 171); "*Megh ke samaan mukta varsha sa jeevan daan, surya ke samaan kamna nadiyon ko pachaate huye seema se baahar na jaana, yahi to Brahman ka adarsh hai*" (4.6 p. 173). But this is all rhetorics and has never been put into practice. Indeed, the main thrust of the drama is to establish the supremacy of Brahmanism and perpetual subordination of the *Shudras*: "*Samay aa gaya hai ki Shudra rajsinghasan se hataye jaayen aur sachche kshatriya moordhabhikshit ho*" (1.5. p. 67). The very genesis of the drama can be attributed to this ideology. Whatever may be historical fact, heavens would not have fallen if Chandragupta, the Shudra would have become the emperor of Arya Vratt. But Prasad's intention was palpably not to set the historic record straight—he was not a qualified historian. The controversy of Chandragupta's lineage still persists. Not merely that. In the drama, choicest invectives like 'dog' have been reserved for shudras (1.5 pp. 68 and 76) the familiar refrain of *Manu Smriti*.

The Bengali drama, on the other hand, made a trenchant criticism of the inegalitarian features of Hindu society, albeit recognizing that "*Kshama, titiksha aur tyag*" (forgiveness, tolerance and sacrifice) are the ideals of Brahman. The play does not favour rigidity in social hierarchy and preaches what Keshab Chand Sen, Vivekanand, Sri Aurobindo had conceived that "essentially there was between the devout Brahman and the devout shudra, no inequality in the single *Virat purusha* (Cosmic spirit)."[19] Vivekanand predicted a "rising of the shudra class with their Shudrahood. . . When the Shudras of every country. . . . Remaining as shudras will gain absolute supremacy in every society."[20]

The Bengali drama has at a number of places reminded the Shudra status of Chandragupta (the Hindi Play has done just the opposite). The play has shown the absurdity and grotesqueness of hatred towards Shudras: "*Chandragupta: Shudra kya manushya nahin hai? Kya kshatriya ke samaan hi iske bhi haath per nahin hai? Mastishk nahin hai? Hridya nahin hai? . . . Itni ghrina!! . . . Dikhaaoonga ki shudra bhi manushya hai*" (Is shudra not a human being? Has he not hands, legs like kshatriya? A mind? A heart? . . . so much hatred. . . . I shall show you that Shudra, too, is a human being" (1.4 p. 23). This reminds us of Shakespeare's "Hath not a Jew eye" dialogue.

Again note this argument: "*Mura: Nand, kya Shudrani ka dugdh kshatriyani ke dugdh se kam madhur hota hai? Kya Shudrani ka sneh kshatriyani ke sneh se kam shubhra hota hai?*" (3.6 p. 75) (Nand, is Shudrani's breast milk less sweet than that of kshatriyani's? Is her affection less warm to kshatriya?) Through Chhaya, the tribal girl, the hollowness and hypocrisy of *Varna*-hierarchy is exposed and ridiculed: "*Chhaya (Chandragupta ko): Ishwar ne aap logon ke shareer ke upar do-char koonchi rang aur pot diya hai. Usi ahenkaar me aap log dharti par per nahin rakhte*" (3.5 p. 72). Not merely that. The poor tribals are presented superior to the 'dwij' insofar as norms or morality are concerned: "*Chhaya: Maharaj, hum deen pahari log hai, hum upkaar ka krey-vikrey nahin karte, hum log uch pravitiyon ka vyavsaye nahin karte*" (3.5. p. 71).

Not only does the Bengali play show the ascendancy of Shudra to the throne, it also disapproves discrimination on the basis of caste, colour and creed. The play underlines the worth of intrinsic human qualities:

Antigonus: *Jab koi mujhse poochta hai ki mera pita kaun hai, aur main koi uttar nahin de pata, to log 'jaaraj' kehkar ghrinapoorvak door rakhte hain. . . apne janm ke liye mera koi daayitva nahin hai, main to karyon ke liye uttardayee hoon . . . kya tumne kabhi mujhko neech karm karte huye dekha hai* (2.3 p. 42) (When someone asks about my father, I fail to answer and they call me 'bastard,' but I cannot be held responsible for my birth. I am accountable for my actions. Have you ever seen me doing base things)?

And furthermore: "*Selucus (Chandragupta ko): Apni putri ka vivah main aapke saath nahin kar sakta, kyonki aap hindu hai/ Helen: Hindu bhi maanav hain.*" (5.1. p. 110) (Selucus: I can't agree to solemnize the marriage of my daughter to you since you are a Hindu/Helen: Hindus too are human beings.)

Gender Perspectives

According to August Bebel, woman was "the first human being to come into bondage. She was a slave before the male slave existed."[21] In the case of Hindu society, her subordination was brought about through ideology of *stridharma* or *pativratadharma* by which women accepted and even aspired to chastity and wifely fidelity as the highest expression of their selfhood. The actual mechanisms and institutions of control over women's sexuality, and the subordination of women, was thus completely invisibilised and with it patriarchy was firmly established as an ideology since it was 'naturalised.'[22] The nineteenth century witnessed furious debates between the liberal reformers and the Hindu orthodoxy over women's bondage.[23] As a result many of the obnoxious and inhuman practices were banned through legislation. With Bankim's *Anandmath* and

Swadeshi nationalism, "mother" emerged as patriotic icon calling sons to the path of self-sacrificing action.

As it turns out, the ideological position of the plays is distanced from the rigidity of the Hindu orthodoxy. But it is the patriarchal framework in which the women have been provided 'autonomous' space which can be curtailed by male authority: "*Is samay naari ki vinti sunne ka samay nahin hai*" (Roy's *Chandragupta*, 2.1, p. 34) "*Chhokriyon se baat karne ka samay nahin hai*" (Prasad's *Chandragupta*, 2.4 p. 105).

The Notion of Marriage

The accent of both the plays is laid on love rather on a higher form of love: "the unification of two souls." Helen and Cornelia express it in these words: "*Naari ka samast jeevan hi prem ka itihas hai*" (Roy's *Chandragupta*, 5.4 p. 124); "*Yahi (prem) stri-jeevan ka satya hai*" (Prasad's *Chandragupta*, 4.9, p. 188). But the question is whether it is equally binding on both the partners? The other related questions are: whether the women can independently take decision about the choice of their life partner? Are they permitted to violate the norms of chastity? It is in pursuit of answers of these questions that one finds that it is the male authority which ultimately has the final say.

The Bengali play shows that the elite were polygamous—the ordeal of Mura and the mother of Antigonus was fruit of such a 'love.' They are the victims of the norms laid down in the Hindu texts, the wife cannot leave the husband but the husband may leave her. Helen is, indeed, indoctrinated by the ideology of 'love' to the extent:

> *Naari ka . . . pehle mata pita, phir pati aur phir santaan—inhi se uska chhota sa sansaar banta hai, yahin par uski aasha vishwas, aanand aur sampatti hai . . . sneh, purush ke vishram ka pramod hai . . . sneh mein hi naari ka janam,*

> *ram ka pramod hai . . . sneh mein hi naari ka janam, niwas aur mrityu hai. Mrityu ke pashchat yadi kahin swarag hai, to weh sneh hi naari ka swarag hai.* (5.4. p. 124)

It is an outright man's world-view, Manu's code which prescribes that "In childhood a woman must be subject to her father, in youth to her husband and when her lord is dead, to her sons. A woman must never be independent." A woman's business, according to Manu, is to her husband to worship him as God. It is *pativrata dharma* which has made women like Helen to believe that it is the duty of a wife to bear with fortitude and a smile all suffering and indignity, the greater the suffering, the greater the glory.

The ideology of wifely fidelity apart, the play has the message of male value of "must-have-a son" which enables them to gain immortality, which is again articulated by Manu: "The production of children, the nurture of those born, and the daily life of men, of these matters the wife is visibly the cause. Offspring, the due performance of religious rights, faithful service and heavenly bliss for the ancestors and for oneself depend on the wife alone."[24] In the drama, it is through Katyayan that the ideology is articulated:

> *Tum kaise samjhoge Nand, santaan ke nimmit vridh pita ki vyatha ko. Jis samay saara sansaar andhakar mein lupt ho jata hai, us samay is lok ka bhavishay—yeh putra hi pita ke netron ke samaksh, aalok bankar prastut hota hai. Pita ke pass kirti-akirti, sampatti-daridrya, paap-punya is jagat mein to kuch bhi hai us samast ko weh putra ke liye chhor jaata hain.* (3.2 p. 60)

In Prasad's *Chandragupta*, the relationship between the husband and wife is conceived in this way: "*Dhaniyon ke pramod ka kata-chhata huya shobha-vraksha. Koi daali ullaas se aage barhi, kutar di gayee. Maali ke man se san-*

ware huye gol-matol khare raho" (4.9. p. 188). In other words what it means is that a wife is a mere appendage of the male, a showpiece with no relevance. Prasad has probably hinted at the conditions of women in the eyes of the wealthy persons. But the redeeming thing is that she realizes the inequitable dispensation which is the pre-condition for turning women themselves into instruments of change.

The gender asymmetry, however, shows some improvement in both the plays and endows individuality and living space. The women are free to make love before marriage, they are not passive; they have been associated with public affairs (in Prasad's play, women take active part in politics and national awakening) they are free to choose/reject their life partners; they shun polygamy (e.g. Alka and Chhaya); and they are bold enough to fight back sexual attempts on their chastity (e.g. Kalyani, Cornelia, Helen, Alka). Yet insofar as the solemnization of their marriage is concerned, the ultimate decision-making authority vests with—rather they themselves have given it to—menfolk, the consent of their father/brother is the final arbiter. This is in line with the traditional thinking that parents are better equipped to handle the vital question of security than an immature girl.

The ideology of chastity and self-restraint has been upheld. For instance, even Suvasini, the courtesan, never allows herself to 'go astray': "*Main Nand ki vilas-lila ka kshudra upkaran bankar nahin rehna chahti*" (1.4 p. 60); "*Maharaj! Main amatya Rakshas ki dharohar hoon. Samraat ki bhogya nahin ban sakti*" (3.5 p. 139); "*Amatya! main anaath thi, jeevika ke liye maine chahe kuch bhi kiya ho; par stritva nahin becha*" (4.2. p. 161). While the women live up to the ideal notion of chastity, this is not the case with males: they are intolerant of the very idea of 'illicit' relation of their 'beloved.' Chanakya employs this ploy to create rift between Rakshas and Nand. Nand, too, is suspicious about Suvasini's love for Chanakya.

When a woman of the status of Suvasini is not a flirt, those belonging to the privileged class like Cornelia, Kalyani, Alka and Malvika have never allowed their chastity to be outraged by anyone. The same norms of chastity have been imbibed by the women in the Bengali play. The mother of Antigonus, despite being deserted in the prime of her youth by her husband, prefers to face alone the ordeals of life. Similar is the case with Mura. Chhaya's story is still more classical: not only was her love for Chandragupta platonic, the idea of choosing her life partner did not occur to her even once though her future with Chandragupta was doomed.

Ideology of Motherhood

The concept of motherhood has come under close scrutiny by feminists. Motherhood involves suffering and deprivations for most women under patriarchy. Indeed, it has been argued by some that maternity is the keystone of the most diverse social and political systems of male control.[25] Under the existing system, the prime time for Indian women was—and is—mature motherhood, because the mother-son emotional bond is closer than any other relationship (who else but the mother knows her son best). After all, all mothers's most cherished desire is to feel proud and happy with their children. That is the supreme reward of motherhood. Patriarchy, whether in its more traditional or modern form, constantly tries to glorify motherhood as the most prized vocation for women.[26]

In Bengal, in particular, motherhood has a deeply ingrained cultural connotation. Bengalis are accustomed to the worship of a variety of female cults. Besides, the burgeoning nationalism in colonial Bengal of the last quarter of the nineteenth century caught hold of the image of mother to represent the nationalist aspirations.[27]

In the image of motherhood, woman is conceptualized as the country itself—*bharat mata, desh mata, dharti maa* etc. This concept of motherhood was the dominant strain in the nationalist discourse from about 1880s down to Gandhian times. Prasad's *Chandragupta* has depicted this artifact of the concept of motherhood (which we have discussed elsewhere). There is no mother character in the play. The Bengali drama has given enormous importance to the ideological aspect of motherhood and has depicted the pain and suffering of a mother.

Both Mura and the mother of Antigonus are examples of suffering and indignity under patriarchy. Both come from the underprivileged strata and develop relationship with royal persons and thereby become mothers. While Mura was concubine; Selucus, husband of the mother of Antigonus, entered into wedlock clandestinely and later deserted her. It is the offsprings of these unfortunate mothers, Chandragupta and Antigonus who, along with their mothers, undergo the worst humiliation for no fault on their part. It is this seamy side of the brahminical patriarchy that has been depicted in the Bengali play.

First, Antigonus and his mother. He is called a bastard because he does not know his father; he is rejected on this very ground by Helen and her father (who, ironically, was also his father). Desperate as he was, he goes to his mother to ask her about his father. And when he comes to know the reality, it stuns him. The poignant depiction of the bleeding heart of a mother and her emotional outbursts are in fact an indictment of the cruelty on women under patriarchy:

> *Antigonus: Ma, Mujhko kshama kar. Main tumhare prati ati kathor ho gayaa tha. . . . Abhagini Ma. Mata: Nahin kewal unke liye abhagini athwa parityakta kewal unke liye. Tere liye main kewal 'Ma' hoon. Tu ek baar phir mujhko 'Ma' kehkar pukar. . . . Sab kasht, sab yantrana bhool jaati hoon. . . . Kewal tera bol sunkar. Antigonus: Tum rajmahishi ho, phir bhi tumhari yeh dasha hai, Ma! Mata: Kewal Ma, Kewal Ma. Aur kuch nahin. Aur kuch nahin. Mujhko 'Ma' kehkar pukar 'Ma' kehhar bol. Antigonus: Meri ma. Mata: Aur ek baar. Aur ek baar. Antigonus: Yeh kya? Tumhare per kaamp rahe hai. . . . Chal Ma tu lait jaa, main teri charan-seva karta hoon, Ma. Antigonus: Ma. Mata: Yahin swarag hai, Mera swarag ghoom raha hai. (4.3 p. 99)*

Mura, the mother of Chandragupta, brought up Nand as her stepson, Chandragupta being elder, was entitled to the throne. But Nand was after his blood. What she says to Nand shows the depth of a mother's love for her child: "*Mera Chandragupta bhikshuk hi bana rahe, parantoo weh jeevit bacha rahe. Mein . . . kewal ek baar apni god mein betha kar khulkar rona chahti hoon. Main Chandragupta ki Ma hoon. . . . Yahi gaurav mere liye bahut hai. Us-se barhkar aur koi doosra gaurav mujhe nahin chahiye*" (1.3 p. 19). And what does the glory of motherhood mean is expressed by Chanakya:

> *Mata—jiske ang ke saath santaan ek din jurhi rethti hai, ek pran, ek man, ek shwas, ek aatma. . . . Mata, jo rog mein, shok mein, denya mein, durdin mein, tumhare dukh ko apne hridya mein dharan karti rahi, jo tumhare mlan mukh ko ujlwal dekhne ke liye apne pran bhi de sakti hai. . . . Mata, jiski apaar shubhra karuna maanav-jeevan ke prabhav mein suryoday ke samaan aalok pradan karti hai, jo santaan ke liye apna sarvasva nichhawar karne mein kriparnata nahin karti. . . . Jo pratidaan nahin chahti. Jo poori shakti se santaan ke hit mein apne ko vileen kar deti hai, yeh . . . maata hai.* (2.5. p. 52)

This suggests that women are by nature devoted mothers which has an ideological underpinning: "we cannot separate the sexual division of labour from sexual inequality. The sexual division of labour and women's responsibility for child care are linked to and generate male dominance."[28] The mother-son relationship apart, the Bengali play has depicted mother in the spiritual image, an aspect which has been discussed under the title "Shakta Ideology.'

The 'Karma' Ideology

The influence of *Bhagavad Gita* and the karma doctrine is very explicit in the Bengali play from the beginning to the end. For instance, when Chanakya is overwhelmed and disturbed over the kidnapping of his daughter, Katyayan consoles him in these words: "*Ye ghatayen chhat jayengee. Ekaki bhetkar nishfal shok mat karo. Nutan udhyog mein kamar kaso. Apne ko karm mein laga do. Is karm-maye sansaar mein thak-kar bethe rehne se kaam nahin chalta*" (1.2 p. 12). And when Chandragupta dithers and refuses to fight Nand, his brother, faces Arjun-like dilemma and asks Chanakya: "*Gurudev, aap kya bhai ka virodh karne ki aagya dete hain?*" Chanakya reminds him: "*Haan, dharamyudh mein, Bhagwan Shri Krishan ne kaha hai.*" And when this argument cuts no ice, Chanakya resorts to Lord Krishna's style, and motivates him (2.5, pp. 50-53).

The 'Karma' ideology is again put forth through the song of beggar and his child, "*Yeh kaisa swar chala aa raha saagar ke us paar se*" (5.2 p. 166) and the subsequent comments by Katyayan: "*tatpurushah samanadhikaranpadah karamdharayah, arthaat wahin par ek purush prakriti ke saath samguranvit hokar arthat jeevbhaav se janm grehn karke, karm dhaaran karta hai—karmafal ka bhog karta hai*" (5.2 p. 117). Even all chance events are just as much governed by the law of karma hence: "*niyati ke samaan durnivar*" (1.1 p. 4)

Prasad's drama is not so explicit on "Karma" doctrine but it has its strain: Shaktar's belief that "*Niyati samraaton se prabal hoti hai*" (3.9. p. 153) (It may also be due to the influence Shaivite theory). Chanakya's exhortation to Parvateshwar: "*Asambhav kehkar kisi kaam ko karne se pehle karm kshetra mein kaamp kar larkharao mat Porav!*" (3.2 p. 128); and Chandragupta: "*Pita gaye, mata gayee, Gurudev gaye, Kandhe se kandha milakar pran dene wala chir-sehchar Simharan gayaa to bhi Chandragupta ko rehna parega*" (4.5. p. 172); "*Jaagran ka arth hai karmkshetra mein avtirn hona. Aur karmkshetra kya hai? Jeevan Sangram*" (4.5 p. 170).

The theory of transmigration, which is also closely linked with doctrine of karma has been propagated by Dandayan: "*Tum . . . mere sharer ko le jaa sakte ho, meri swatantra aatma par tumhare dev putra ka bhi adhikar nahin ho sakta*" (1.11. p. 85).

Shakta Ideology

An image of resurgent and fearful strength irrevocably is associated in the Bengali mind with the concept of Shakti. A number of female deities are worshipped in Bengal. Similarly, tantricism down the centuries has provided a crucially important 'underside' to Hindu religious tradition in Bengal. It constitutes the doctrinal core of Shakta practices. Ramkrishan Paramhansa contributed to make Shakti worship much more respectable and widespread among western educated middle class groups. The Bengali play has shown it too abundantly, Chanakya is always invoking: "*he vibhatse, bhagvati vasundhare! He adrishya Mahashakti, 'Pishachi'*" and so on. And similarly Chhaya invokes Shakti: "*Maheshwari! Jis shaktibal se tumne daanavon par jai praapt ki thi, usi ka ek kann mujhko dene ki kripa karo*" (2.4. pp. 44-46). The song "ratri bhayavah, andhkar se aavrita dharii ambar" (4.1. p. 86) is devoted to shakti.

Philosophy of Joy and Bliss

Prasad's outlook on life was very much influenced by Aryan's anandvad (blissfulness) and Kashmir's Shaivite philosophy of *Prityabhijya darshan*. As a votary of the past, he thought that *anadvad* was an integral part on the life pattern of Aryans: "*Kintu Prachin Arya log sadeiv se apne kriya kalaap mein aanand, ullaas aur pramod ke upaasak rahe. . . . Mahavir Indra aatmvaad aur aanand ke pracharak the. . . . Vedic sahitya mein . . . urvashi aadi apsarayon ka jo prasang hai weh uske aanand ke anukool hi hai.*"[29] Chandragupta shows this ideology at a number of places, for instance, "*Rakshas: Suvasini . . . main is kshanik jeevan ki ghariyon ko sukhi banane ka pakshpaati hoon. Aur tum jaante ho ki maine byah nahin kiya, parantoo bhikshoo bhi na ban saka*" (1.4 p. 60); "*Simharan: Ateet sukhon ke liye soch kyon, anaagat bhavishya ke liye bhay kyon aur vartmaan ko apne anukool bana hi loonga phir chinta kis baat ki*" (1.1.p. 52).

The Ideology of Patriotism and Nationalism

Under the influence of the nationalist discourse, the concept of the motherland (*deshmata*) dominated the literary works from about 1880s down to Gandhian times: the country is not a piece of land with actual people living in it. It is abstracted from the people and is then personified as the Mother Goddess, the most sacred deity in the Hindu pantheon. The people then are not 'desh' itself, but are sons of the Mother, detached from the imagined entity and put in a subordinate relation to it. Emotional resonances connected with an enslaved mother-figure tended to be particularly powerful for arousing the masses.

The 'invader-invaded' framework provides ample scope—rather raison d'être—for arousing patriotic sentiments. The Hindi drama is cast in this framework in which Chanakya and Chandragupta organize the native feuding satraps against the Greek invaders and defend and strengthen the 'nation' of Aryavratta. The Bengali play has underlined the perspective when it dwells on the concept of just war which we have dealt with elsewhere. Therefore, unlike the Bengali play, the Hindi drama's constant refrain is the defence of '*Rashtra*' (nation and patriotism): "*Chandragupta: Atmasamman ke liye mar mitna hi divya jeevan hai*" (1.1. p. 50); "*Simharan: Janambhoomi ke liye hi yeh jeevan hai, jab aap-si-sukumarian iski sewa mein katibadh hain, tab main peeche kab rahoonga*" (1.6. p. 71); "*Chanakya: Smaran rakhna hoga ki ishwar ne sab manushyon ko swatantra utpan kiya hai*" (3.9. p. 157) (Remember, God has created all men free)—it is reminiscent of Tilak's 'Freedom is my birthright.' The central argument of Chanakya's political philosophy is the establishment of a sovereign state of Greater India.[30] "*Malav aur Magadh ko bhoolkar jab tum Aryavratta ka naam loge, tabhi weh milega*" (1.1 p. 51) (You can achieve the goal only when you forget about Malav and Magadh and think in terms of Aryavratta); "*Yavan aakramankaari Bodh aur Brahman ka bedh na rakhenge*" (1.5 p. 66) (the invaders will not make a distinction between the Brahmans and the Buddhists). The colonial "divide and rule" policy has been articulated as "*Yeh sidhant viheen, nrishansa, kabhi bodhon ka pakshpaati, kabhi vedicon ka anuyayee bankar dono mein bhedneeti chalakar bal sanchay karta rehta hai.*

Moorkh janta dharm ki aut mein nachayee ja rahi hai" (1.4. p. 62).

The play has recreated the scenario of mass upsurge of the 1920s at the call of Gandhi against the British when both men and women plunged into the liberation struggle. Alka is cast in the paradigm of a '*virangana.*' Totally imbued with patriotism, she revolts against her brother, Ambhik, and joins Chandragupta, Chanakya and Simharan: "*Yeh mera desh hai mere pahar hai, meri nadiyan hain aur mere jungle hain, is bhoomi ki ek ek parmaanu mere hain aur mere shareer ke ek ek kshudra ansh inhi parmaanuyon ke bane hain*" (1.10. p. 81); "*paradheenta se barhkar vidambna aur kaya hai*" (2.7. p. 116). Not merely that. She leads the masses and exhorts them: "*Taxila ke veer naagrikon. . . . Aryavratta—pyara desh—Greekon ki vijai laalsa se poonah paddalit hone jaa raha hai. Jab tumhara shasak tatasth hone ka dhong karke punya bhoomi ko partantrata ki sharankhla pehchanne ka drashya raajmahal ke jharokhon se dekhega*" (4.5. p. 176). And the battle cry: "*Himadri tunga srigna se/Prabudha shudha Bharti/Swayam prabha samujala/Swatanrata pukarti*" (4.6. p. 177).

Strikingly, the Hindi play has used the term 'nation' as if the Indian nation has been in existence right from Vedic/ Mauryan age which is a historic fallacy that arose in the course of the anti-colonial movement itself.

Discourse on Hinduism and Buddhism

Patanjali, the grammarian, has referred to the hostility between Brahmanism and Srimanism as innate as is that between the snake and the mongoose.[31] These two religious groups had different sets of beliefs and rituals and often disagreed on social norms. That this distinction was recognized is evident from the edicts of the Mauryan king

Ashoka and the accounts of Megasthenes, Fa Hsien, Hsuan Tsang and Alberuni.[32]

Prasad's play has dwelt on the polemics between these two groups but the manner in which the play has presented shows bias for Hinduism. The play has glorified the tenets and values of Brahmanism through Chanakya, Dandayan and Varruchi: "*Brahman sab kuch saamarthya rakhne par bhi, swechha se in maaya-stoopon ko thukra deta hai, parkriti ke kalyan ke liye apne gyan ka daan deta hai*" (1.1. p. 48); "*Brahman ha bhai ! tyag aur kshama ke pramaan*" (1.7. p. 73); "*Megh ke samaan varsh-sa jeevan daan, surya ke samaan abadh vikeern karna, saagar ke samaan kaa-mna—nadiyon ko pachaate huye seema ke baahar na jaana; yahi to Brahman ka aadarsh hai*" (4.6. p. 180). In contradiction to this, Buddhism has been portrayed with a different brush. Mark what the play says about Buddhism: "Buddhism is the religion for the whores" (1.4 p. 60). Brahman Rakshas tells Suvasini: "*Main swaym hridya se Bodh mat ka smarthak hoon; kewal uski daarshnik seema tak*" (1.4 p. 60); and "*Bodh dharm ki shiksha maanav vyavhar ke liye poorn nahin ho sakti, bhale hi weh sangh vihar mein rehne waalon ke liye upyuqt ho*" (1.5 p. 65).

The Doctrine of Liberty

Another salient feature of the Hindi drama relates to its espousal of the doctrine of liberty. The slogan of the French Revolution was "Liberty, Equality and Fraternity." The American Declaration of Independence also embodied the same ideas. Perhaps taking a cue from these historical events, Chanakya exhorts the citizens of Magadh following the overthrow of Nand in the same vein: "*Magadh ke swa-tantra naagrikon ko badhaayi hai. Aaj aap logon ke Rash-tra ka janm-divas hai smaran rakhna hoga ki ishwar ne sab manushyon ko swatantra utpann kiya hai, parantoo vyaktigat swatantrata wahin tak di jaa sakti hai jahan doosron ki swatantrata mein badha na pare. Yahi rashtriya niyamon ka mool hai*" (3.9. p. 157). Chanakya's 'God has all men free' reminds Rousseau's 'Man is born free.' The play underlines that the notion of liberty does not envisage to encroach upon the freedom of others. What is, however, striking is that out of the three words of the French Revolution, the play has shown its concern for ushering in the era of 'Liberty.' But in a society with legitimized and institutionalized inequality ingrained in the caste system, 'liberty' is meaningless for those at the receiving end of the system.

The Theme of Hunger

The Bengali play has recreated the horrors of famine and the sufferings it heaped on the wretched of the earth. The mother of Antigonus, one of those unfortunates who during the days of such calamity were compelled to sell even their offspring just to buy one meal, has been chosen to depict the picture.

How devastating the event turned out both for the mother and the son has been poignantly depicted in the play. While Antigonus constantly has to bear the indignity of being dubbed a bastard in society, it has equally been traumatic to his mother. Antigonus expresses his agony: "*Tum kaise samjhogi us maansik vyadhi ki marm peera ko, jiske vyang se vikshipt hokar main askash se toot-te huye taare ke samaan prithvi par chakkar kaat ta phirta hoon. . . . (Mata hokar) ek muthi ann ke liye pashu ke samaan haat mein apni santaan ko bech diya*" (4.4 pp. 76-77) (Being a mother, you sold in the market your progeny like an animal for the sake of a handful of grain).

And what drove her mother to the desperate act and what the nightmarish trauma she experienced afterwards is recounted in these words:

> *Tum kaise samjhoge vats! Kshudha ki jwala kaisi hoti hai jiski maar se paagal hokar maine is prakaar ka karya kiya tha. . . . parantoo uske pashchaat kitne deergh divason aur kitni nidraheen raaton ka maine apne ashrujal se abhishek kiya hai. . . . main teri is bhook ka smarn karti thi aur mere netron ke saamne ka sansaar lupt ho jaata tha. Jo ann main mukh mein daalti thi weh meri ushna nishwason ke taap se bhasm ho jaata tha. . . . Kshudha ki jwala kaisi hoti hai yeh tu kaise samjhega. Kaise samjhega!!* (4.4. p. 96)

In fact, the nineteenth century India was struck by 31 famines with an estimated total of over 21.5 million deaths.[33] Hunter's *The Annals of Rural Bengal* (1868) has described the horrors of the Bengal famine of 1770, in which one-third of its populations had perished.

All through the stifling summer of 1770 the people went on dying. The men sold their cattle, they sold their implements of agriculture, they devoured their seed grain, they sold their sons and daughters, till at length no buyer of children could be found, they ate the leaves of trees and the grass of the field, and in June 1770 the Resident of the Darbar affirmed that the living were feeding on the dead. Day and night a torrent of famished and disease stricken wretches poured into great cities.[34]

Although Roy, being himself a sub-divisional officer, could have seen the appalling conditions of the Bengal peasants and indigent masses with his own eyes, it is the description in Hunter's report that has been captured in his play. The description, however, exposes the insensitiveness of the colonial masters towards subjugated people of India.

Notion of Rightful Self-Defence and Just War

The Bengali drama propagates the ideology of just war. While it holds war in general as a 'trade in murders,' "*Yudh to hatya ka vyavsaya hai*" (4.3. p. 94), it makes a distinction between just and unjust wars. It approves war when it is demanded by *dharma* waged in self-defence. For instance, Chandragutpa's war with Nand was a *dharma* war to end a tyrannical rule. Likewise, war is justified when "*Akraanti desh ko bachane ke liye, agnidah, vinaash aur lootmaar se desh ki raksha karne ke liye shanti ki shubra pataka ko ooncha rakhne ke liye*" (4.3 pp. 94-95). In fact, war waged in the defence of peace is moral: "*Helen Yadi aatmaraksha ke liye yudh aavashyak hai to avashya kiya jaye, kyon ki doosra upaay hi kya hai. Yudh shanti ki raksha ke liye he shaanti bhang karne ke liye nahin*" (4.3. p. 95).

In Bengal it was Bankim who had advanced this notion in *Krishna Charitra* (1886): "It is moral to wage war in defence of myself and of others. To shy away from doing so is grave immorality. We, the people of Bengal, are bearing the consequences of our immorality for seven hundred years."[35]

The Hindi drama does not put forth the concept of just war. There is, however, a remark made by Chanakya which disfavours war without valid grounds: "*Tum logon ko samay par shastra ka prayog karna parega. Parantoo akaaran raktpaat neeti-virudh hai*" (1.1. p. 50).

Ideology of Humanism

Although, Prasad's *Chandragupta* attacks colonial war of annexation and pleads for peace and harmony, the Bengali play's accent on humanism and peace is more pronounced. Dandayan proclaims that "*Hatya, rakt-paat aur agnikand ke liye upkaran jutaane mein mujhe aanand nahi*" (1.11. p. 87). Cornelia recounts the horrors of war more eloquently "*Wahi Bharatvarsh. . . . Ab hatya aur loot se vibhatsa banaaya jaayega. Greek sainik is shasya shyamal prithvi ko rakt-ranjit banaayenge. . . . Pishachi ki chhalna mein padkar laakhon praaniyon ka naash hoga*" (4.7. p. 182). The Bengali drama perceives "*Jo shanti ke kshetra ke upar raktpaat ki dhaara bahana chahte hain weh . . . samagra maanavjaati ka shatru hai, weh niyam aur vyvastha ka shatru hai, dharm ka shatru hai*" (4.3. pp. 93-94); "*sekaron maataaon ko putraheen, balikaon ko pitraheen, satiyon ko patiheen bana dena desh mein aatank jaga dena. . . . Kewal vijay ka gaurav praapt karne ke liye. . . . Is se barhkar aur kaun sa paap ho sakta hai*" (5.1. pp. 108-9).

The play has noted the building up of tensions and gathering of war clouds over Europe when in their scramble for markets, the colonial powers had forged two antagonistic blocks—the Triple Alliance (1882) and the Triple Entente (1907). The play notes this development: "*Hinsa apne sahastra phano ko phelakar dauri aa rahi hai aur weh sansaar mugdh drashti se uski aur dekh raha hai*" (4.3. p. 95) and that "*Is vishwas-parivaar ko vidwesh aur ahenkaar ne jis prakaar ek-doosre se prathak kar diya hai, us prakaar se nadi parvaton ne nahin kiya*" (4.3. p. 95); "*manushya lobh ke kaaran vicharheen hinsa mein lipt hokar ek doosre ki gardan mein daant garaye huye hai*" (2.5. p. 47).

Not only does the play indict the forces threatening world peace and abhor predatory wars, it highlights the need to wipe the perennial problems of hunger, disease and ignorance off the face of the earth: "*Helen: Dukhi ka dukh door karna, rogi ki seva karna, bhooke ko bhojan dena, agyani ko gyan prapt karaana. . . . In sab mein se kya kuch bhi nahin hai? Kewal swarthparta, hinsavriti, atyaachaar, avichaar, vinash hi shesh bacha hai?*" (2.1. p. 28).

Conclusion

Both the plays have attempted to seek answers from the cultural resources of Hinduism. The construction of India's past is influenced by Eurocentric outlook and nationalist discourse which was the ideological climate during the nineteenth and early twentieth century. But there are other influences too, the playwrights' predilections, vision and belief system.

Hindi drama, written in the 1920s, bears the impact of Gandhian nationalism also. The theory of Aryan Race and uniqueness of Indian culture is the underlying ideology of both the plays. But there is a divergence in their perception of the scheme of things: while both the plays envisage a Brahminical framework as the answer for India's malaise, the Hindi drama tends to favour *varna*-system. The Bengali play is less rigid about the victims of the *varna*-system. The Shudras are endowed with more living space. The Hindi play has depicted the brighter side of Hinduism in its polemics with Buddhism. The Hindi drama, woven in the invader-invaded framework is punctuated with sentiments of nationalism and patriotism, albeit the concept of 'nation' as depicted in the play is ahistoric, rather "rhetorical prejudice" according to which the Indian nation had existed even in the Mauryan Age. The gender question has been presented from the patriarchal perspectives in both the plays, but here again there is a difference. The Hindi play allows relatively more freedom to the women while the Bengali drama has the strains of Manu's dictums. The motherhood has been presented in both the plays but with a difference. The Bengali play has depicted the harsh treatment meted out to mother under patriarchy, the emotional bonds between mother and her offspring, the Hindi drama has used the concept of "Motherland." In the Bengali play, the Archetypal Mother is invoked which testifies to the influences of Shakti ideology. Prasad's drama shows the influence of the ideology of *Anandvad.* The Bengali drama propagated, in loud terms, the *Karma* ideology of *Bhagavad Gita.* While both the plays have decried war of aggression and espoused causes of peace, the Bengali play has underlined the concept of just war. The refrain of Roy's drama is universal peace, brotherhood and elimination of perennial problems of hunger, disease and ignorance—the banes of humanity.

NOTES

1. Pierre Viar, "The Age of Don Quixote," p. 68.
2. Amilcar Cabral, "Return to the Sources: Selected Speeches of Amilcar Cabral," p. 63. Cited K.N. Pannikkar, "Culture and Ideology: Contradictions in Intellectual Transformation of Colonial Society in India," p. 2115.
3. Amilcar Cabral, "Unite et Lutte," p. 44. Cited Patrick Chabal, *Amilcar Cabral: Revolutionary Leadership and People's War*, p. 183.
4. Preface of *Vishakh.*
5. Preface to Roy's *Chandragupta.*
6. M.G.S. Narayanan, "Historical Perspectives on Ancient India," p. 3.
7. For example, the Gupta Age has often been described as 'Golden Age.' All those 'golden features' could be seen in the Kushan Empire, but the Kushan were left out. Perhaps, they were considered mlechhas, unclean foreigners. See Avjit Pathak, *History, Science and Identity*, p. 30.
8. Romila Thapar, *Interpreting Early India*, especially essays 1, 2, 4, and 5, also her *The Past and Prejudice.*

9. For example, the Greek society which was erected on murky foundations of slavery was also eulogized the same way, "Some historians anxious to present the glory that was Greece, in the most favourable light, have discounted the part played by slave labour and even declared that Greek society was not a slave society." George Thomson, *Studies in Ancient Greek Society,* p. 197.
10. G.J. Deshpande, "The Kingdom of Darkness or the Problem of Culture," p. 1865.
11. J.D.M. Derret, *Essays in Classical and Modern Hindu Law,* p. viii.
12. Jyotiba Phule, the founder of Satyashodhak Samaj (Truth-seekers' society), in 1873 came out with a scathing attack on the Theory of Aryan Race and Brahmanism.
13. Cited from Aijaz Ahmad, "Fascism and National Culture: Reading Gramsci in the Days of Hindutva," *Social Scientist,* p. 48.
14. Sisir Kumar Das, *The Artist in Chains: The Life of Bankim Chandra Chatterjee*, pp. 212-13.
15. Sumit Sarkar, *Modern India.*
16. Compare this with "Fountain of human light, the apex of human civilization, the exemplar of courage and humanity, the perfection of good Government and settled society, the mother of all religions, the teacher of all wisdom and philosophy. It has suffered much at the hands of inferior civilizations and more savage peoples . . . its pride has been trampled into the dust and its glory has departed." Qtd. Sri Aurobindo, *India's Rebirth*, p. 28.
17. Qtd. F. Franco and Sarvar V. Sherry Chand, "Ideology as social practices: The functioning of *Varna*," p. 2606.
18. Qtd. Jwala Prasad Chaturvedi, *Manu Smriti*, p. 25.
19. Sri Aurobindo, *India's Rebirth.*
20. Qtd. Sumit Sarkar, 'Kaliyuga,' 'Chakri,' and 'Bhakti, p. 1564.
21. August Bebel, *Women under Socialism*, p. 9.

22. Uma Chakravati, "Conceptualizing Brahmanical Patriarchy in Early India," pp. 582-83.
23. See Tanika Sarkar, "Rhetoric against Age of Consent," pp. 1869-78.
24. Manu, X, 26-27.
25. Adrienne Rich, *Of Woman Born: Motherhood as Experience and Institution*.
26. Jasodhara Bagchi, "Representing Nationalism: Ideology of Motherhood in Colonial Bengal."
27. *Ibid*.
28. Nancy B. Chadorow, "The Reproduction of Mothering: Psychoanalysis and the Sociology of Gender," qtd. Charu Gupta, "Portrayal of Women in Premchand's Stories," p. 92.
29. Jayshankar Prasad, "Rahasyavaad," *Kavya aur kala tatha anya nibandh*, pp. 49-50.
30. Roy's Chanakya has the same dream.
31. Qtd. Romila Thapar, *Interpreting Early India*, p. 62.
32. *Ibid*, p. 63.
33. R.P. Dutt, *India Today*, p. 129.
34. Qtd. Sisir Kumar Das, p. 130.
35. Qtd. Partha Chatterjee, "Transferring a Political Theory: Early Nationalist Thought in India," p. 126.

Bibliography

Works on Prasad

Bhatnagar, Ramratan. *Prasad ka Jeevan aur Sahitya.* Delhi: Rajdhani Prakashan.

Chakravarti, Uma and Kumkum Roy. "In Search of our Past: A Review of the Limitations and Possibilities of the Historiography of Women in Early India," *Economic and Political Weekly,* Vol. XXVIII, No. 18 (1988), pp. ws-2-10.

Chatak, Govind. *Prasad: Natya Aur Rang Shilpa.* Delhi: Atma Ram, 1969.

———. *Prasad ke Natak: Swaroop aur Sanrachna.* Delhi: Sahitya Bharti, 1975.

———. *Prasad ke Natak: Srijnatmak Dharatal Aur Bhashik Chetna.* Delhi: Atma Ram, 1972.

Dhananjaya. *Prasad ke Aitihasik Natak.* Allahabad: Smriti Prakashan, 1970.

Gupta, Parmeshwari Lal. *Prasad Ke Natak.* Varanasi: Hindi Pracharak Pustakalaya, 1956.

Gupta, Krishnanand. *Prasad ke Do Natak.* Lucknow: Ganga Pustak Mala Karyalaya, Sam. 1998.

Joshi, Jagdish Chandra. *Prasad ke Natakon ka Aitihasik evam Sanskritik Vivechan.* Delhi: Atma Ram, 1970.

Khaneja, Ramesh Kumari. *Prasad Yugeen Natak.* New Delhi: Taxila Prakashan, 1981.

Madaan, Indra Nath, ed. *Prasad Pratibha.* Delhi: National Publishing House, 1971.

Manav, Bishambar. *Prasad ke Paanch Natak.* Allahabad: Kitab Mahal, 1974.

Nagendra, ed., *Jayshankar Prasad: His Mind and Art.* Delhi: Prabhat Publication, 1989.

Paliwal, Rita Rani. *Rangmanch Aur Jayshankar Prasad ke Natak.* Delhi: Sahitya Nidhi, 1984.

Pota, Nirupma. *Prasad ke Natakon ka Manovaigyanik Adhyayan.* Allahabad: Abhinav Bharti, 1974.

Prasad, Jayshankar. *Kavya aur Kala tatha anya Nibandh.* Allahabad: Bharti Bhandar, Sam. 2005.

Sharma, Jaganath Prasad. *Prasad ke Natakon ka Shastriya Adhyayan.* Varanasi: Saraswati Mandir. 7th edn. Sam. 2028.

Shilimukh, Ramkrishna. *Prasad ki Natya Kala.* Moradabad: Manas Mukta Karyalaya, 1930.

Shukla, Bhanudev. *Prasad ka Natya Sahitya.* Meerut: Meenakshi Prakashan.

Shukla, Bhagwati Prasad. *Prasad Yugeen Natak.* Bhopal: Madhya Pradesh Hindi Granth Akademi, 1971.

Tandon, Premnarayan, *Prasad ke Teen Natak.* Bangalore: Vidya Mandir, 1974.

Thakur, Devesh. *Prasad ka Naari Charitra.* Delhi: Navyug Prakashan.

Vajpayee, Nand Dulare. *Jayshankar Prasad.* Allahabad: Leader Press, Sam. 2020.

Vyas, Vinod Shankar. *Prasad aur unka Sahitya.* Banaras: Hindi Sahitya Kutir, Sam. 2006.

Works on Hindi and Bengali Literature

Chattopadhyaya, Jayanti. "The Rise and Fall of Chandragupta: The Hindi Response to Dwijendralal Roy," Amiya Dev and Sisir Kumar Das, ed. *Comparative Literature: Theory and Practice.* New Delhi: Allied, 1989.

Chatterji, Suniti Kumar. "The Origin and Development of the Bengali Language," Calcutta University, 1926.

Das, Sisir Kumar. *The Artist in Chains: The Life of Bankim Chandra Chatterji.* New Delhi: New Statesman Publishing Co., 1984.

De, Sushil Kumar. "Bengali Literature in the Nineteenth Century" (1757-1857). 1962.

Ghosh, J.C. *Bengali Literature.* London: O.U.P., 1949.

Gupta, Manmath Nath. *Bangla Sahitya Darshan*. Delhi: Sasta Sahitya Mandal, 1960.

Gupta, Rama Sen. *Hindi tatha Bangla Natakon ka Tulnatmak Adhyayan*. Indore: Kamal Prakashan, 1971.

Maheshwar. *Hindi Bangla Natak*. Macmillan, 1974.

Shukla, Ramchander. *Hindi Sahitya ka Itihas*. Kashi: Nagari Pracharini Sabha, 11th edn., Sam. 2014.

Literary Criticism

Choudhry, I.N.. "Pradesa in Hindi Chhayavad and After," *Indian Literature*, Vol. XXVII, No. 2 (1984) pp. 56-66.

Dev, Amiya and Sisir Kumar Das, ed. *Comparative Literature: Theory and Practice*. New Delhi: Allied, 1989.

George, K.M. *Contemporary Indian Literature*. Madras: Kerala Sahitya Akademi & Macmillan, Vol. 1984.

Gupta, Somnath. *Hindi Natak Sahitya ka Itihas*. Allahabad: Hindi Bhawan, 1958.

Joshi, Svati, ed. *Rethinking English: Essays in Literature, Language, History*. New Delhi: Trianka, 1991.

Kusumkaar. *Hindi Natya Chintan*. Delhi, 1971.

Majumdar, Swapan. *Comparative Literature: Indian Dimensions*. Calcutta: Papyrus, 1987.

Malik, Shanti. *Hindi Natakon ki Shilp Vidhi ka Vikas*. Delhi: National Publishing House, 1971.

Mali, Shiv Ram. *Swachhandata wadi Natak aur Manovigyan*. Kanpur: Pustak Sansthaan, 1976.

Misra, Jagdish Prasad. *Shakespeare's Impact on Hindi Literature*. New Delhi: Munshiram Manoharlal, 1970.

Misra, Lakshmi Narayan. *Mukti ka Rahasya*. Varanasi; Parijaat Press, 1964.

Misra, Vishwanath. *Hindi Natak par Paschatya Prabhav*. Allahabad: Lok Bharti, 1966.

Mohammed Malik. *Hindi Sahitya ko Pradeshon ki den*. New Delhi: Rajpal, 1977.

Nagendra. *Adhunik Hindi Natak*. Agra: Sahitya Ratna Bhandaar, 1960.

——, ed. *Bhartiya Natya Sahitya.* Delhi: S. Chand, 1978.

Narayana, Birendra. *Hindi Drama and Stage.* Delhi: Bansal, 1981.

Ojha, Dasarath. *Hindi Natak: Udbhav aur Vikas.* Delhi: Rajpal, 5th edn., 1970.

Ojha, Mandhatta. *Hindi Natya Samalochna.* Delhi: Rajpal, 1976.

Prawer, S.S. *Comparative Literary Studies.* New York: Barnes and Noble, 1973.

Purohit, Shanti Gopal. *Hindi Natakon ka Vikasatmak Adhyayan.* Dehradun: Sahitya Sadan, 1964.

Rai, Amrit. *A House Divided: The Origin and Development of Hindi. Delhi:* Oxford University Press, 1984.

Rai, Gulab. *Hindi Natya Vimarsh.* Lahore: Meharchand Laxman Das, 1943.

Rao, S. Balu. "Tradition and Experiment in Indian Literature," *Indian Literature*, Vol. XXXII, No. 2 (1989), pp. 143-54.

Sen, Priyaranjan. *Western Influence in Bengali Literature.* Calcutta, 1947.

Sharma, Ram Vilas. *Mahavir Prasad Dwivedi aur Hindi Navjagran.* Delhi: Rajkamal Prakashan, 1977.

Sharma, Sripati. *Hindi Natakon par Pashchatya Prabhav.* Agra: Vinod Pustak Bhandar, 1961.

Singh, Bachchan. *Hindi Natak.* Allahabad: Lok Bharti Prakashan, 1975.

Singh, Udayabhanu. *Chhayaavad.* Delhi: Saamaik Prakashan.

Swarup, Savitri. *Navya Hindi Natak.* 1967.

Taneja, Satyendra. *Hindi Natak: Punarmulyankan.* Kanpur; Grantham, 1971.

Tyagi, Kailash Chandra. "Dwijendralal Roy aur Prasad ke Natakon ka Tulnatmak Adhyan. Unpublished Ph.D. Thesis, Meerut University, 1971.

Varshney, Lakshmi Sagar. *Adhunik Hindi Sahitya.* Prayag: Hindi Parishad, 1947.

Vimal, Ved Pal Khanna, *Hindi Natak Sahitya ka Alochanatmak Adhyayan.* Delhi: Sri Bharat Bharti (Pvt Ltd.). 1958.

Williams, Raynold. *Keywords.* Fontana: Croom Helm, 1977.

Socio-Political Background

Acharya, Pormesh. "Development of Modern Language Text-Books and the Social Context in 19th Century Bengal," *Economic and Political Weekly*, Vol. XXI, No. 17 (1986), pp. 745-51.

Ahmad, Aijaz. "Fascism and National Culture: Reading Gramsci in the days of Hindutva," *Social Scientist*, No. 38-39 (1993).

Antonovo, K.A., et al. *A History of India in Hindi.* Moscow: Pragati Prakashan, IInd edn., 1988.

Aurobindo. *India's Rebirth.* Paris: Institut de Recherches Evolutives, 1907.

Bebel, August. *Women under Socialism.* New York: Schocken Books, 1971.

Chabal, Patrick. *Amilcar Cabral: Revolutionary Leadership and People's War*. Cambridge: Cambridge University.

Chodorow, Nancy B. *The Reproduction of Mothering: Psychoanalysis and the Sociology of Gender.* Berkeley: University of California Press, 1978.

Chakravati, Uma. "Conceptualising Brahmanical Patriarchy in Early India," *Economic and Political Weekly*, Vol. XXVIII, No. 24 (1993), pp. 579-85.

Chandra, Sudhir. "Literature and the Colonial Connection," *Social Scientist*, 121 (1983), pp. 3-47.

Chatterjee, Partha. "Transferring a Political Theory; Early Nationalist Thought in India," *Economic and Political Weekly*, Vol. XX, No. 3.

Chaturvedi, Jwala Prasad. *Manu Smriti.* Haridwar, 1992.

Derret, J.D.M. *Essays in Classical and Modem Law*, Vol. III, Leiden, 1977.

Deshpande, G.P. "Dialectics of Defeat: Reflections on Literature. Theatre and Music in Colonial India," *Economic and Political Weekly*, Vol. XXII, No. 58 (1987), pp. 2170-76.

Dutt, R.P. *India Today*, Calcutta: Manisha, 1989.

Gupta, Charu. "Portrayal of Women in Premchand's Stories," *Social Scientist*, No. 216-17 (1991).

Franco, F. and Sarvar V. Sherry Chand. "Ideology as Social Practices: The Functioning of *Varna*," *Economic and Political Weekly*, Vol. XXIV, No. 47 (1989).

Jaffrelot, Christophe. "Hindu Nationalism: Strategic Syncretism in Ideology Building," *Economic and Political Weekly*, Vol. XXVIII, No. 12 & 13 (1993), pp. 517-24.

"'Kaliyug', 'Chakri' and 'Bhakti,'" *Economic and Political Weekly*, Vol. XXVII, No. 29 (1992), pp. 1543-66.

Kumar, Krishna. "Quest for Self Identity: Cultural Consciousness and Education in Hindi Religion (1880-1950)," *Economic and Political Weekly*, Vol XXV, No. 23(1990), pp. 1247-55.

———. "Hindu Revivalism and Education in North-Central India," *Social Scientist*, Vol. 18, No. 10 (1990), pp. 4-26.

Macaulay. "Minute on Indian Education," *Prose and Poetry*, Selected by G.M. Young. Cambridge, M.A.: Harvard University Press, 1967, p. 729.

Mookerji, R.K. *Chandragupta Maurya and His Times*. Delhi: Motilal Banarsi Das, 1966.

Narayanan, M.G.S. "Historical Perspectives in Ancient India," *Social Scientist*, Vol. IV, No. 5 (1975).

Niranjana, Tejaswini. "Translation, Colonialism and Rise of English," *Economic and Political Weekly*, Vol. XXV, No. 15 (1990), pp. 773-79.

Pathak, Avjit. "History, Science and Identity," *Mainstream*, 16th October 1993.

Ray, Bharti. "Women of Bengal: Transformation in Ideas and Ideals (1900-47)," *Social Scientist*, No. 216-217 (1991), pp. 3-23.

"Review of Women Studies: Ideology of Motherhood," *Economic and Political Weekly*, Vol. XXV, No. 42-43 (1990).

"Rhetoric against Age of Consent," *Economic and Political Weekly*, Vol. XXVIII, No. 36 (1993), pp. 1869-78

Rich, Adrienne. *Of Woman Born: Motherhood as Experience and Institution*. New York, 1976.

Sarkar, Sushoban. *On the Bengali Renaissance.* Calcutta: Papyrus, 1979.

Sarkar, Tanika. "Nationalist Iconography: Image of Women in 19th Century Bengali Literature," *Economic and Political Weekly*, Vol. XXII, No. 47 (1987), pp. 2011-15.

Sastri, K.A. Nilakanta, ed. *Age of Nandas and Mauryas.* Delhi: Motilal Banarsi Das, rpt. 1988.

Sarkar, Sumit. *Modern India (1885-1947).* Macmillan, 1985.

Singh, Jasodhara. "Representing Nationalism: Ideological of Motherhood in Colonial Bengal," *Economic and Political Weekly*, Vol. XXV, No. 42-43, WS-65.

Srimali, Krishna Mohan. "Religion, Ideology and Society," *Social Scientist*, Vol.16, No. 12 (1988), pp. 14-60.

Srivastava, Mukesh. "Mosaic of Narrative Manipulation; Power and Production of Subjectivity," *Economic and Political Weekly*, Vol. XXVII, No. 4 (1992), pp. 47-57,

Thapar, Romila. *Interpreting Early India.* Delhi: O.U.P., 1993.

———. "The Perennial Aryans," *Seminar. No.* 400 (1992).

Thomson, George. *Studies in Ancient Greek Society.*

Trevelyan, Charles. *On the Education of the People of India.* London: Orme Brown, Green and Longman, 1838.

Texts Cited

Prasad, Jayshankar. *Chandragupta.* Allahabad: Bharti Bhandar (20th edn), 1972.

Roy, Dwijendralal. *Chandragupta Natak.* Trans. Om Prakash. Delhi: Pitamber, 1987.

Visakhadatta. *The Mudrarakshas.* Trans. M.R. Kale. Delhi: Moti Lal Banarasi Das, 1965.